SIMEON SOLOMON

COLLECTED WRITINGS

EDITED AND WITH AN INTRODUCTION BY
DANIEL CORRICK

SIMEON SOLOMON (1840–1905), born in London to a prominent Jewish family, was a Pre-Raphaelite painter who first exhibited at the Royal Academy in 1858. In 1873 he was arrested and then convicted for attempted sodomy, an event which curtailed his ability to show his work, though it was still collected by such notable figures as Oscar Wilde and Count Eric Stenbock. He wrote a number of short works, including the extended prose poem "A Vision of Love Revealed in Sleep" (1871).

DANIEL CORRICK is an editor and literary historian with a specialist interest in nineteenth-century literature, especially the evolution of Gothicism and the Decadent movement. He has worked on a number of volumes including the collected fiction of Montague Summers, and unpublished works of Edgar Saltus and Edward Heron-Allen. In addition, he has edited several anthologies, including *Sorcery and Sanctity: A Homage to Arthur Machen* (Hieroglyphic Press, 2013), and *Drowning in Beauty: The Neo-Decadent Anthology* (Snuggly Books, 2018).

CONTENTS

INTRODUCTION

OVER the last few decades there has been a considerable revival of interest in the work of the Pre-Raphaelite artist Simeon Solomon. This is partly due to a greater appreciation of his more unorthodox later work and because of the unique combination of queer and Jewish symbolism employed throughout his career. For a considerable period, he was mentioned primarily as a cautionary footnote to the sadomasochistic proclivities of his former friend Algernon Charles Swinburne, and or as a cult figure in the history of Victorian homosexual counter-culture, a sort of precursor to Wilde and the Uranian poets. Much of the early work to better evaluate Solomon's reputation as an artist was undertaken by the British art historian Lionel Lambourne, who wrote essays on him and his siblings, Abraham and Rebecca. A biography, also by Lambourne, was written but failed to appear due to lack of a publisher. By the start of the 1990s appreciation for Solomon as an artist and for his place in the history of Aestheticism had picked up, partly as a result of the critical foundations laid by Lambourne and professor Gayle Seymour in her 1986 thesis *The Life and Work of Simeon Solomon (1840-1905)*. In 2001 the London Jewish Museum featured an exhibition dedicated to his work, followed three years later, on the centennial of the artist's death, by a major retrospective at the Birmingham Museum and Art Gallery. Since the onset of the digital age, his admirers have built a considerable web presence in the form of the Simeon Solomon Research Archive.

Unlike William Morris or Dante Gabriel Rossetti, who thought of themselves as poets as well as visual artists, Solomon seldom made use of the literary medium. The only prose work of his known to the public was the prose poem "A Vision of Love Revealed in Sleep", a mystical allegory told in pseudo-Scriptural style. Most of the other items from his pen are now vanishingly rare, often limited to a single copy preserved in specialist archives. I have chosen to present these alongside Solomon's letters to Swinburne leading up to the publication of his prose poem and three reviews of the that piece, one from the poet himself, another anonymous, and a third from the critic and prominent theorist of homosexual *eros* in art, John Addington Symonds; in doing so the reader may get an idea of the tone of Solomon's life prior to and after writing, as well as the guarded way in which it was received.

The majority of the artist's additional works are satirical in tone, either having been intended for small private audiences or—possibly—for publication anonymously or under a pseudonym. For a man who wrote little Solomon has had a surprisingly diverse range of materials attributed to him from Sunday School lectures to the infamous gay pornographic novel *Sin of the Cities of the Plain*. The majority of these attributions are either spurious, as in the case of the aforementioned novel, or doomed to remain speculative in case of the lectures.

The artist's first known literary foray was supposedly a novel written in his early twenties. It has not survived though a series of sketches intended as illustrations are still with us. They show a rather broad clownish sense of humour, which was to be a mark of his personality throughout his life, as evinced by his correspondences and anecdotes from friends. From around the same period there are several sketches depicting whimsical caricatures of himself drawn in the style of the black and white illustrations which adorned the pages of then popular serialised novels. Over forty years later the same self-satirising tendency shows itself strongly in a para-graph-long mock autobiography, "A History of Simeon Solomon, From the Cradle to His Grave", he provided for Julia Ellsworth Ford's monograph *Simeon Solomon: An Appreciation*. It is likely that such a jocular mode of self-depiction, including as it did a certain ambiguity towards his Jewish heritage, bespoke a long-lasting un-certainty about his own self-image. In the same essay he describes himself as "so disgraceful that his family . . . would have nothing to do with him"; yet existing evidence shows this not to have been the case, although a downturn in the family's fortune prevented his more distant relatives from providing financial aid towards the later part of his life. Certainly both his parents continued to support him and his sister Rebekah till the end of their lives, and a cousin stood bail for him when in 1873 he was arrested for soliciting in public toilets and attempted sodomy. Likewise, nothing gives cause to believe that Solomon became persona non grata in the Jewish community, the scandal of his arrest being—unlike that of Wilde—a matter of private rather than public knowledge, though understandably his co-religionists preferred his earlier Old Testament work to the Symbolist imagery of his latter period. However, by the time of his financial difficulties in the mid-1870s the artist exaggerated and embraced his purported pariah status as a perverse form of self-justification.

Another very early comic item was "The P.R.B. Catechism for the use of the disciples of that School", written in 1859 right around the time at which the artist made the acquaintance of Dante Gabriele Rossetti. It was a mock manifesto of Pre-Raphaelite aesthetics and ideals, poking fun at various perceived traits such as the supposed mania for red haired models and fanatical veneration of Ruskin's aesthetic theory, as well attacking "those of the Slosh", an in-house derivate for members of the British Academy. The original manuscript, once the property of Henry Holiday, was sold at Christie's on the 20th of July 1983 and the current writer has been unable to trace its whereabouts. We owe the few excerpts that remain to Gayle Seymour who quotes in her *The Life and Work of Simeon Solomon (1840-1905)*. Although light-hearted in tone it would have been social advantageous move on the young Solomon's part; in writing such a thing he was declaring affiliation with the movement, yet the elements of parody would obviate any claim to be speaking for the more established members.

A surviving example of the artist's comic writing is the short pamphlet entitled "Two Treatises on Scientific Subjects", which the artist privately commissioned through the well-known London printing firm Spottiswoode & Co, who were also to produce the prototypical "Mystery of Love in Sleep". It was published in 1871 but had its origins at some point in the early 1860s as a piece recited to friends and relatives at social gatherings. It survives as a single copy once belonging to the English poet Frederick Locker-Lampson, who left it to posterity with exclamatory note. *"This pamphlet was given to me by a poor wretch called Simeon Solomon. I knew him in Rome & then he was esteemed a young man of exceeding promise but he has a vicious, morbid style & did not advance in reputation & one day he was obliged to hide himself & he has never been seen since—tho' I believe he is alive & in London. Swinburne adored his art. He had a brother and sister who also painted."*

The treatises themselves are short spoofs of the scientific lectures popularised in the early part of the nineteenth century by Michael Faraday and continued by far less illustrious figures. Solomon makes broad fun of the pompous and worthy style of the self-proclaimed "scientific educator", with remarks like "in the dark ages the ignorant imagined the earth to have been square". From their brevity they were evidently intended to be read out loud. The title page lists a number of other titles supposedly from the same author. Given their farcical nature one assumes that they too are merely part of the spoof, though several researchers have attempted to locate them. The Oxford scholar Lewis Roberts makes the intriguing suggestion that a series of pamphlets signed "Ancient Simeon", published in the 1870s and 1880s by the London Sunday School Union, could be in fact the "Moral Lectures" there mentioned[1]. Upon inspecting these I am unconvinced, for although a few of them e.g. "Talks About Walks" or "Grumbling Cured— Gratis" bear some resemblance to his known works in terms of style and humour, the circumstances and rather Puritanical tone of the publication would make Solomon's authorship most incongruous[2]. Even if we are to accept that Solomon's enthusiasm for Christianity amounted to formal conversion, the form of heavily ritualistic, aestheticised Catholicism he showed sympathy for could hardly have commended itself to an organisation as avowedly Dissenter as the Sunday School Union.

Another item the authorship of which has long been attributed to Solomon but never proven is the anonymous play, "Cleopatra's Needle", published in 1877.

---

1 Roberts discusses this possibility in his article "The Lost Letters" published on *The Oxford Review of Books* website.
2 Many of these purported items are collected together in a book entitled *Pleasant Papers* published in 1887, though said volume states they were originally published in periodicals decades before.

As no contemporary reviews exist and the script was never submitted for approval to the Lord Chamberlin's Registrar we can safely assume it was never performed at any major theatre. A single copy exists as part of the British Library's Ashley Library collection, a veritable treasure-trove of manuscript and correspondence of Pre-Raphaelite material which also hosts Solomon's correspondence with Swinburne. Authorship was ascribed to Solomon by the original compiler of the Ashley collection, Thomas James Wise, who attached it to one of the artist's letters, as he had done with two of his other publications. Unfortunately, Wise, who enjoyed a great and undoubtedly deserved reputation as a scholar and bibliographic authority during his lifetime, is now equally remembered for his criminality after it was discovered that a number of the rare, first edition publications he had "recorded" were in fact forgeries. In the case of "Cleopatra's Needle" however no mention of it is made in any of it in his bibliographies nor was there ever any attempt made to sell the item, so little motive can be found for deceitful as opposed to potentially erroneous ascription. Both Seymour and Lambourne are prepared to consider it as one of Solomon's creations, though caution that its true pedigree will most likely never be known.

In terms of content the play is a broad farce of miserly relatives, mistaken identities and absurd situations. The humour is similar to Solomon's other comic items, but then again so was popular stage humour at the time. A few circumstantial facts in favour of authorship, namely, that Solomon's mother had an architect as one of her lodgers during the years immediately before the play was written, and that Sir Erasmus Wilson, the man responsible for the transport of the actual London Obelisk, was a close friend of one of Solomon's patrons[1]. It has been argued that the parodic, at one point overtly anti-Semitic, depiction of the two East European Jewish bailiffs tell against his having written it, but as anecdotes show Solomon was both willing to make self-depreciating jokes about his Jewish heritage in order to entertain friends, and to emphasise his perceived "Hebrew" status to better sell paintings, it does not tax belief that he should play on popular prejudices if he thought it was in his financial interests to do so.

Solomon's major work of prose, the only one written as a serious accompaniment to his paintings, was the long prose poem "A Vision of Love Revealed in Sleep". A century and a half since its publication it is looked on rightly as one of the major works of Pre-Raphaelite prose and of Victorian queer spiritual autobiography. The prototypical version of the piece was written during a visit to Rome in 1870, and printed as a short pamphlet under the title "A Mystery of Love in Sleep" by Spottiswood early the following year. Although ostensibly an allegory, that of an unnamed first person narrator being guided by

---

1 I owe this point to the discussion of the play's authorship in Dr. Caroyln Conroy's *He Hath Mingled with the Ungodly: The Life of Simeon Solomon After 1873, With a Survey of the Extant Works*, 2009. Dr. Conroy is one of the architects of the Simeon Solomon Research Archive.

an aspect of his spirit to witness the ruin and glorification of Love personified as a divine youth, the piece is primarily a succession of beautiful tableaux, the proximate inspiration for which are a series of the artist's paintings depicting beautiful androgynous figures including *Bacchus* (1867), *Love in Autumn* (1867), *Amor Sacramentum* (1868), *Love in Death* (1870), *Dawn* (1870) and *Love Dreaming by the Sea* (1871). Solomon's main stylistic influence is probably the sensualised quasi-medievalism of Rossetti's poetry, though he borrows heavily in both idiom and imagery from the Biblical Song of Songs in such a way as would appeal to those who looked upon him as a "Hebrew" artist. The publication, however, was not released to the reading public, and were it not for the republication it might well have lapsed into the same obscurity as the "Lectures".

Later that year Solomon revised and released an expanded version of the piece under the title of "A Vision of Love Revealed in Sleep". Unique amongst the artist's writings, this book appeared as a bound volume, with Solomon also designing the cover image and interior decoration. The publisher, F.S. Ellis, was a mainstay of Pre-Raphaelites, having published material from Swinburne in addition to both collections of Rossetti's verse; although in the case of "Vision" the colophon displays some ambiguity as to whether it was part of Ellis' catalogue proper or just produced and sold by him at Solomon's bequest. It has been suggested that such reticence might have reflected some misgivings about the contents of the piece, but given that Ellis was to publish Swinburne's notoriously in-flammatory *Songs Before Sunrise* that same year I do not believe this plausible. More likely it represented a commercial arrangement between the two parties on which Solomon paid part of the printing costs.

The frontispiece contains a sepia reproduction of an original sketch undertaken by Solomon, showing two figures in half-portrait, one in a pilgrim's garb, the other haloed and bearing a blossoming sprig, both recognisably male but with the fine features and full lips beloved of Pre-Raphaelite portraiture. They are intended to represent the protagonist and his guide Spirit but Solomon was fully aware that on first sight they would remind the viewer forcibly of Virgil and Dante at the opening of the *Inferno*. The initial sketches for this picture were undertaken in 1869 and it has been suggested that they served as the impetus for the prose piece rather than vice versa.

The text had been extended to almost three times its original length. Solomon's addition of a framing device and clearer narrative structure improves the piece considerately, transforming it from a phantasmagoric dream vision to an allegorical journey after the manner of the *Divine Comedy*. Scriptural imagery occupies a more prominent place in this revision, particularly Love as the suffering Christ. The latter depictions of Love wounded near unto death by Passion and bound to a tree could not fail to recall the famous depictions of Saint Sebastian throughout classical art.

Much has been written on the symbolism and purpose of the piece from both the perspective of sexology and mysticism. Although there is an obvious temptation to interpret depictions of the tortured masculine body in Victorian art as an expression of frustration at sociological bounds it would be more fruitful to understand it in terms of the positive, or at least necessary, roles that physical suffering and *extremis* play in the expression of both sexuality and religious devotion. As far as we know despite a few joking references to canning in his correspondence Solomon lacked the severe sexual preoccupation with pain that coloured Swinburne's work, defying simplistic attempts to explain this away in terms of masochism. Suffering is considered almost by definition a passive happening, but the process of an agent's suffering does involve activity and thus may serve as a form of expression, possibly of expressing meanings beyond the fact that one is in pain. In reading "Vision" as a coded reflection on the sexual aspects of his being what is expressed is the experience of desire itself rather than desire for someone. Although Solomon had sexual, or at least erotic, encounters with men which shaped the course of his life, there is little evidence to suggest that he ever had much in the way of a long term romantic relationship with another man—absent from most of his work is that yearning for that "special friend" which characterises much of Victorian queer poetry.

As well as being one of the major works of Pre-Raphaelite aestheticism in prose, its subject and imagery made contributions towards the nascent Decadent movement. Intimations of homosexuality as some forbidden and tragic but beautiful precisely in its tragedy, an affliction or aberration that conferred some suffering spiritual nobility, would become increasingly more overt in poetry through the last part of the nineteenth century, ceasing in England (though not on the continent) at the trial of Oscar Wilde. Depictions of beautiful youths somnambulant and delirious amidst heaps of poppies were common from classical mythology but would have gained further dubious connotations following increasing public awareness of the recreational potential of narcotics. As well as homoerotic martyrdom imagery the figure of the androgyne would also become prominent in *fin-de-siècle* art, this time as a mystical symbol representing the completeness of the new man who transcends and synthesises the beauty in both sexes.

Solomon was eager to ensure a favourable reception for his creation upon its release, importuning Swinburne on the basis of their old friendship to review it for the newly established literary journal *The Dark Blue*. The first discussion of the piece however was an anonymous review in the March 25th issue of *The Athenaeum*, closely by another from Symonds in *The Academy* at the beginning of the next month. Not until July did Swinburne's review appear. All three reviews praise for the poem for the beauty of its imagery and stress the centrality of Solomon's paintings to properly appreciating its story, though both the poet and the unnamed writer for *The Athenaeum* lament the lack of further illustrations, suggesting, delicately in the case of the former and frankly in the latter, that more narrative substance was required to prevent it from merely being a succession of gorgeous imagery.

Solomon evidently was not pleased with Swinburne's gentle criticism and complained to him about it in their correspondence. The exact nature of these complaints are unknown as Swinburne's side of the correspondence has been lost, his letters allegedly having been sold by the then-impoverished Solomon several years later, an event, or rumoured event, which earnt him the enduring hostility of the poet, who by this point was beginning to regret his youthful boastings of perversity and earnestly hoped no more of them would come to light. It is not my intention to discuss the range of Solomon's surviving letters here. One can only hope that the future will see a further volume colleting together correspondence with Rossetti, Burne-Jones, Pater, Oscar Browning and others. It was decided, however, to include the artist's letters to Swinburne as contained in the Ashley Library collection, as they provide insight into the publication of "Vision" and how it was received, as well as glimpses into the writers' shared interest in erotica. Edmund Gosse, whose propensity for literary arson was to lead to the destruction of Arthur Symonds papers, urged Wise to destroy them, for they contained evidence that Swinburne was aware of Solomon's "notorious vices". To modern readers Solomon's side at least sounds rather mild. The humour is schoolboyish and one might find it ironic that a private mention of *Peter Spy*, a racy penny-dreadful newspaper later banned, should frighten Swinburne, the man Wilde had called "braggart when it came to vice", given the fact that he himself had chosen to quote de Sade, although not by name, in the aforementioned review ("the philosopher of the material school"—the quote that follows is from *Juliette*).

The lack of Swinburne's side of the correspondence is also regrettable, for it touches on one of the most famous critical discussions of Solomon's art in the context of Pre-Raphaelite literature. This is of course Robert Buchanan's "The Fleshly School of Poetry", a fierce polemic against the sensuality and perceived unwholesome quality the movement had introduced into verse originally published in the October 1871 issue of *The Contemporary Review* under the pseudonym "Thomas Maitland". Though primarily an attack on Rossetti Buchannan also directs his ire at Solomon, who he accuses of lending "actual genius to worthless subjects, and thereby produce veritable monsters—like the lovely devils that danced round Saint Anthony". Interestingly it was the supposed indecent portal of heterosexual lust in Solomon's work and not the androgyny of his figures or the homoerotic undertones which earned him this criticism. Swinburne suspected Buchanan was the author of the piece initially, a belief which Solomon for reasons unknown did not share and communicated as such to the poet in his letters, temporarily delaying his and Rossetti's ill-advised retaliations. Swinburne retaliated a year later with his own polemic "Under the Microscope" but Solomon remained silent and there is no sign he felt any deep wound to his self-image.

"A Vision of Love Revealed in Sleep" was Solomon's great attempt at artistic self-justification in prose. Although it lacks that narrative assuredness that Morris and Rossetti's prose possessed, the piece, and the serious of paintings which inspired it, present an aesthetic strikingly different from the sensualised medievalism that typified Pre-Raphaelite art and the Neo-Hellenism that would predominate queer poetry of the period. In a sense his unexplained blending of gender in the case of angelic or divine figures is bolder than Swinburne's obvious attempts at provocation. None-the-less it is the first and last of its kind; the artist would never again attempt to elucidate the meaning of his paintings, even such a highly allegorical form. No further works of prose signed with Solomon's name were to appear.

Whether Solomon was to write anything further is a question for future literary detective work to solve. The bouts of extreme poverty he was to experience in the lasts decades of his life made the acquisition of any additional income a necessity rather than a choice, and it is hard to imagine that a man forced to sell the scandalous correspondence of his once friend would have qualms about writing a few paragraphs for a magazine. There is a reason to doubt he did so, however. Although anonymity might not be out of place for a populist stage comedy in the 1870s, by the last part of the twentieth century he would have most likely been able to make more money signing any written work under his own name than anonymously or with a pseudonym. Unlike in the case of

Wilde, whose reputation was destroyed virtually over-night, Solomon's scandals were not public knowledge and his reputation would instead suffer slow erosion due to the incautious words of former friends and the honest testament of those who meet him in the dissipated state of his later life. Even to the end of his life he continued to sign his paintings and sketches with his own name or initials, which shows that it did not devalue them. With this in mind, it is likely that he could have made more from writing anecdotal articles about his memories of Rossetti and the early days of the Brotherhood than any anonymous mate-rial. It is the decades of the 1860s and 1870s that are the most likely candidates for undiscovered work. We can only hope that the manuscript of his lost "P.R.B. Catechism" will come to light again and that further correspondence will reveal more about his eventful life during those periods. The extant material how-ever forms a fascinating note to the career of one of nineteenth century Britain's most unique painters; a career that was marked by precocity and self-doubt, by comradery and uncertainty over identity, by sensu-ality and hardship, and most of all by intense personal expression of beauty.

A NOTE ON THE TEXTS

THE text of "Two Treatises on Scientific Subjects" was taken from the copy held in the Archives and Rare Books Library at the University of Cincinnati. The text of "Cleopatra's Needle" was taken from the copy held in the British Library's Ashley Library collection, as was the correspondence with Algernon Charles Swinburne.

The editor and publisher would also like to thank Professor Gayle Seymour for her comments on the "P.R.B catechism", as well as the staff at Christie's Auction House, the British Library, the Mark Samuels Lasner Collection, and especially Kevin Grace and the University of Cincinnati Archives and Rare Books Library.

COLLECTED WRITINGS

A HISTORY OF SIMEON SOLOMON,
From his Cradle to his Grave

AS an infant he was very fractious. He developed a tendency towards designing. He had a horrid temper. He was hampered. He illustrated the Bible before he was sixteen.

He was hated by all of his family before he was eighteen. He was eighteen at the time he was sent to Paris. His behaviour there was so disgraceful that his family—the Nathans, Solomon, Moses, Cohens, etc., *et hoc genus homo*—would have nothing to do with him. He returned to London to pursue his disgraceful course of Art, wherein he displayed such marvellously exquisite effects of coleography that the world wondered. He then turned his headlong course into another channel—that of illustrating books for youths. His "Vision of Love revealed in Sleep" is too well known. After the publication of this his family repudiated him for ever.

His appearance is as follows: Very slender, dark, a scar on one or two eyebrows, a slouching way with him, a certain nose, one under lip.

That is

S.S.

A MYSTERY OF LOVE IN SLEEP

Ego dormio, et cor meum vigilat
Cant. Cant.

THE form of One stood by me, undraped, save for a fillet binding his head, the ends of which lay upon either side of his neck; also upon his left shoulder hung a thin strip of drapery; in his right hand he bore a branch of dark foliage starred, with no blossoms; his face had on it the shadow of the consciousness of glad things unattained, as of one who ever sought but never found, upon whom the burden of humanity lies heavy; his eyes, half shaded by their lashes, gave forth no light. I knew that my Soul stood by me, and he and I went forth together; and I also knew that the visible images of those things which we know only by names were about to be manifested unto me; when I gazed into the lampless eyes of my Soul I felt that I saw into the depths of my own spirit, shadow meeting shadow. We went forth towards a dim sea at ebb, lying under the veil of the mysterious twilight of dawn: on its grey sands sat One whom I knew for Memory; over her face passed the changeful alternations of sun and cloud, shade and shine; the voice of the shell which she held to her ear, unburied the dead cycles of the soul: it sang to her of good and evil things gone by, and her introverted eyes looked upon them as when one looks in a mirror upon all else save oneself. My soul turned his dusky eyes upon me, and then I too heard the voice of the shell, and the ocean cast up my dead before my eyes, and all was to me as though it had not gone by. Memory bore upon her head and breast a light rain of faded leaves and blossom, and upon her raiment small flecks of foam had already dried; her lips trembled with the unuttered voices of the past, but she did not weep. My Soul and I went on gradually ascending a sandy slope, patched here and there with scanty grass, and against the pale sky we saw One, for whom, looking upon, my Soul dissolved in tears, so stricken with the unavailing sorrow was he, so wounded beyond the hope of healing; bound hand and foot, languishing under the weight of his humanity, crushed with the burden of his so great tenderness. I looked upon the face of my Soul, and I knew that he, in whose presence we now stood, was Love, but Love dethroned and captive, bound and wounded, bereft of the natural light of his presence, his wings drooping, broken and torn, his hands made fast to the barren and leafless tree, the myrtles upon his brow withered and falling, and upon that heart, from whose living depths should proceed the voice of the revolving spheres, there was a wound flowing with blood, and changing into roses of the divinest odour as it fell. I stood motionless, my eyes refusing to look longer upon my stricken lord, then drawn unto my Soul from whom I had no comfort; the voice of the shell of Memory yet sounded in my ears, and I knew that the divine captive read my spirit's inmost thoughts; from his proceeded inaudibly the words, "Thou hast wounded my heart."

After a moment of supreme mystical agony, I raised my eyes, and behold! the vision of Love was gone. I looked out to sea, and there came towards us One whose name my Soul told me was Passion, she who had wounded and had sought to slay Love, but who, in her turn, was grievously wounded and tormented in strange and self-devised ways: the glory of her head was changed into the abiding place of serpents whose malice knew no lull, her wasted beauty preyed upon itself, her face was whitened with pale fires, a hollow image of appeased desire, her eyes flowed with unavailing tears; in her right hand she bore a self-wrought sword of flame, and in her left, the goodly fruits and flowers she held were scorched and withered, and crawled upon by evil things; her feet were bound in inextricable folds, she was borne forth she knew not whither, her breath was as the breath of the hungry sea, and rest shall not be given unto her. When I looked upon her, and knew that she would have slain Love, pity was congealed in my heart; then the voice of the shell spoke to me by the spirit, and said, "thou hast no pity on thyself." This vision also passed from us, and my Soul and I yet went forth by the sea until we came upon a temple, whose door being touched by the branch which was borne by my Soul opened, and my spirit yearned for the further mystery which was to be vouchsafed to me. In front of us stood One who had lotos flowers and cypress bound upon his head; he held a lotos flower in his hand, and one finger upon his lip; his face was overshadowed with the mystery of Life, as the face of one who dwells for ever without the Holy Place, upon whose brow the highest radiance has not fallen; by his side lay a crystal globe, into which he might not look; his mien had in it the gentleness of a creature that desires to caress and to be caressed, but dared not approach; his was the pallor of one who had wrestled with another strong as himself, and had prevailed, but whose dominion was hateful to him, whose power was his humiliation, whose strength his weakness. I sought my Soul, and I knew that I was standing before him who had battled with Love, Death, who would love us if he dared, whom we would love if we dared. My Soul now said unto me, "Raise thine eyes and behold," and I saw coming towards us what had the appearance of a bird moving softly along the still, grey air; as it approached us, I perceived two presences, one reclining upon the other, who gently fanned the air with great wings. And now a deep calm fell upon my spirit, such as one feels when the burden of a great trouble is averted, and my Soul and I wept when we saw him who was being thus carried towards us; he lay lightly across the breast of his supporter, cheek reposing against cheek; upon his head were two small fair wings, and round his brow were bound the flowers and buds of poppies; upon his

face there shone a distant light of childhood, his parted lips breathed forth peace; the One who bore him
smiled upon him, and rejoiced because of his burden.
I knew that he who was winged was called Divine
Charity, and his charge Sleep. When we went forth
out of the temple wherein abode Death we came to
a strange land stretching far out towards the wan sea,
and inland the earth was overgrown with rank weeds,
and ever the voice of the shell sounded in my ears, and
the land to the right and left of me seemed to image
my past years; the comfort which I had had of Sleep
departed from me, and when I sought the eyes of my
Soul no rays of consolation came forth there-from, no
blossoms of golden light yet starred the dull branch
he bore: the shadow of the house of Death lay heavy
upon him.

Now again two came towards us, one bearing the
other, and treading down the dark growth of weeds
that thickened about us. When I saw him who reposed in the other's arms, a trembling seized me, and
an awe came upon me—the awe which is begotten
of exceeding pity: around his head shone a faint and
flickering light, his white and perfect body was flecked
here and there with blood, my Soul spoke to me by
the spirit, and I knew that the vision of Love was again
vouchsafed to me, but, as when we saw him by the sea,
betrayed, wounded, and helpless. He who supported
him was ravaged with the storms of ages: in his eyes
there rang the voices of unnumbered years; his mien
had in it a great tenderness of one unconquerable; as a
mother encircles with her arms a beloved and sorrow-

ing child, and softly murmurs to him the songs of his infancy, so he pressed his bruised and smitten charge to his breast, comforting him the universal voice. I covered my eyes as this vision of wounded love in the arms of time passed from us. The earth was now covered with poppies, and the air was heavy with odours, and I would fain have sought Sleep, but that I knew it was forbidden unto me; moreover, it was given to me to know by my Soul, through the spirit, that another mystery was shortly to be vouchsafed unto me. The air was murmurous with faint sounds borne on the odour of the poppies; these were the echoes of the voices of my past years. I again sought the eyes of my Soul, and I saw dimly reflected in them the image of him whom we went forth to meet. I removed my gaze from my Soul's face, and looked abroad, and I beheld, in the pale light of the first stars, Love, seated upon a thrown, lowly and poor, and not worthy to bear him,—no longer, indeed, wounded and bleeding, but still bereft of his perfect glory; in his eyes there shone a soft light of suffering not yet past, but on his brow, where poppies were wound among the living myrtles, there lay the shadow which falls upon one not remembered; upon his parted lips hovered the half-formed smile of a child who halts between weeping and laughter; he was fully clothed in a raiment of dim and sullied red and gold; in one hand he bore a poppy branch mingled with myrtle, from which the stars had fallen one by one, and in the other a golden globe whose brightness was obscured and shamed by dust; his feet were wholly hidden in the thick growth of weeds and poppies that crowded round his throne; he spoke no word, only the faint sounds in the air about him and the grief-dimmed eyes of my Soul told me that he was Love imprisoned in an alien land of oblivion—forgotten, put away.

Our hearts burdened with sorrow's weariness, again we set forth along that mystic land, and as we gazed upward, our vision rested upon One seated; around her burned the light of the new-born stars; whose harmony made glad the pulses of the air; from her wide brow went forth a healing balm, in her aspect all men seek their rest and hide them in her shadow. She bore upon her knees One still beautiful, but pallid with woes, riven with wasting troubles, weary and dying; within her heart she hid his passing spirit; the waning golden light about him faded in the gloom of her hair, the falling blossoms of his head lightly strewed her dusky raiment wherewith she wholly enfolded him; he sank beneath her sacramental kiss, and Day was lulled to death in the all-embracing arms of Night. And now we went forth upon our dimly lighted path, where the red and purple of the poppies faded into sombre grey beneath the faint rays of the lately risen stars, and the depths of the still pools which lay to right and left of us sent up their pale reflections, and ever the utterances of the sea of my life spoke to me by the voice of the shell of Memory; and this night seemed to be a figure of my past. After my spirit had bent itself to the pondering of these things, I turned me towards my Soul, and his eyes were heavy with the sense of a coming mystery. I looked forward, and I saw that

we approached what appeared to be a temple in ruin,
long forsaken and not remembered; its crumbling
marble walls and pillars, worn by time and storms,
glimmered dimly beneath the stars; about it lay the
decayed fragments of its dead beauty, and its entrances
were choked up with poppies and clinging weeds, but
to my spiritual vision there appeared a radiance about
it that made me know that the light of him whom I
sought penetrated the depths of its enduring gloom.
Our heads bowed, and in silence we approached the
entrance; we put aside the rank growths which sought
to hinder our going in, and stood on its grass-gown
threshold; then the silence of my heart was broken by
its weeping, and a faintness fell upon me when I lifted
up my eyes to the vision now revealed to me. Before
us was an altar-like monument carved with a legend
of old-time, whereon the joyful creatures who sported
in procession across were wasting in decay, time-dis-
coloured and riven; upon it he lay, whom, when we
stood in the presence of Death; we saw borne to earth
by Divine Charity; he was wrapped about with the
slumber of those upon whom no shadow has fallen,
upon his face there lay that far-off light of childhood,
the mildness of his half-formed smile drew the spirit
unto itself, his lashes were yet moist with late-shed
tears, born not of sorrow but of tenderness; looking
upon him, our wave-tossed spirits found their haven,
and rest fell upon us. Before I dared to look upon
him who was present with Sleep, and whom I have
not wearied of seeking, I saw by the spirit that one
rose impalpably from the heart of the poppies, and

hovered upon them, lapped in his half-shut wings; his eyes were not covered by their lids, yet it seemed as if slumber had fallen upon them; he fixed his mystic gaze upon a crystal globe he held in both of his hands, wherein I knew by the spirit he saw pass the dreams of those who sleep beneath the stars; his locks were softly lifted by the air, and his lips trembled with the weight of the myriads of visions he called forth; his bent face was overshadowed by the exceeding sadness of one who knows the thoughts of men. Again I raised my eyes, and I saw her who had lately been revealed to us receiving the passing breath of day; she watched his unreleaxing gaze, and eyes from whose depths comes forth all gentleness, Sleep, her beloved son, and she, to whom all was an open scroll, wept when she looked upon him whose heart was as the heart of a little child; her dusky locks flowed forth upon the air, and from their shade the stars sent down their beams; her garments were fragrant with the blossoms begotten of Day's death, and hymns proceeded from the silence that was about her; upon her all-supporting arms, and hidden in her raiment, she bore those who slept and dreamed, and those who watched; she whispered peace unto those who know it not when she is not, she put away from them the sword, and healed the wounds that gape and bleed when she is not by to close them; she drew the spirit of the mother to her child who dwells in far-off lands, and in her arms the long-separated were brought together; beneath her shadow the lost little one yet again nestled upon her mother's breast, she hid the stricken in her heart, by her the forsaken were taken back to the hearts of the forsakers; she brooded over the uncared-for with the soft care of her wings, and by her the forgotten were brought to remembrance.

Then I sought my Soul in trembling, for I knew that there was One present on whom I had not yet dared to look, and my Soul said to me by the spirit, "Behold him whom we seek, but we are not yet prepared." Then I turned my gaze upon him; in the gloom of the unremembered temple he sat in all lowliness upon the fragment of a broken frieze, whereon the sculptured histories of his ancient glory crumbled and fell away, forgotten and uncared for, blighted by the breath of ages, stained with the rust of storms that know no mercy; his red and golden raiment hung loose about his limbs, and the blossoms from his hair had fallen crisped, and dead upon his shoulders, the tears of a Divine agony yet lay upon his cheek, the radiance which I had seen by my spirit before my feet had gained the threshold of the temple sprang from the sound upon his heart, and when I looked upon and saw it illumine the dim eyes of my Soul, my spirit abased itself, and my gaze fell upon the earth; then I knew that this vision had been fulfilled, and my heart, ringing with the inner voices of the things that had been revealed to us, and my eyes laden with their images, I again turned unto my Soul, and I saw that upon his countenance rested the light that came forth of Love's wound, and made it shine; and, as we departed from the temple, I rejoiced secretly at this; also I felt strengthened and gladdened at heart because of

Sleep, and my spirit was softened by reason of his smile, and we turned our steps towards the waning stars. Our course now lay along an upward slope, whereon the poppies waxed scantier and the weeds less rank; a soft mossy grass soothed our wayworn feet, and I could see by the light of the dying stars, that small golden blossoms lay in a pattern upon the sward; as we neared the brow of the hill, I knew that a yet unseen and mysterious presence was about to be revealed to us; soft breezes bore his light to us upon their wings, and voices from the passing Night spoke to us of him; he was half-seated, half-lying upon a height beyond which was stretched out the faintly glimmering sea; there lay upon him yet the shadow of the Night, but his face had upon it the radiance of an expected glory, the light of glad things to come; his eyes were yet soft with the balm of Sleep, but his lips were parted with desire, his breath was as that of blossoms that wake and lift up their heads and give forth their odours, his dusky limbs were drawn up as if in readiness to depart, and his great and goodly wings softly beat the air; with one hand he cast away his dim and dewy mantle from him, and with the other he put aside the poppies that had clustered thickly about him; as he turned his head to the East, the poppies fell from his hair, and the light rested upon his face; the smile it kindled made the East to glow, and Dawn spread forth his wings to meet the new-born day; and when the Day was seated on his throne, we passed along pleasant land that lay beneath the light of a great content, and the radiance yet lingered on the countenance of my Soul, and the sadness that had made the curves of his mouth heavy, and had dimmed his eye, now gradually departed, and there came upon him an aspect of calm as one certain of a good thing shortly to befall, although he knows not fully what it may be; and when I looked upon his eyes my spirit took heart, and I girded myself and set forward with my head no more bent, and we were met by many who had been shown me in my former dreams; and who all bore the reflection of a light upon their faces. And when the throne of day was set well nigh above our heads, and there was that in the air which moves the heart of nature, we rested ourselves beside a running stream, whose waters brought joyous sounds from afar, as it were the long-forgotten songs and gentle voices of our child-hood, yet laden with a heavier and fuller harmony from a source we knew not yet; and as we journeyed on in the dawn of the evening, an awe fell upon me, as when one enters upon a new and unknown way, and all the air about teemed with the echoes of things past, and the vague intimations of things to come. I turned my gaze upon the eyes of my Soul, and I rejoiced greatly through my spirit to see a brighter glow upon them, as from the expected coming the long-desired, and when I cast my eyes upon the earth I discerned there many happy creatures, joyous and beautiful, and such as have no existence in the neighbourhood of evil; after a space, and when my eyes had been gladdened by reason of those things, I again turned them upon my Soul, and I knew that what we sought would now shortly be revealed to us.

A weakness fell upon me, but my Soul supported me; we looked forward, and saw One approaching clothed about with a soft light; he moved towards us, gently lifted by the spirit from the ground, neither flying nor running; ever and again his feet, wherefrom sprang glowing wings, touched the earth and caused it to bring forth flowers; his head was bound with a fillet of violet, and violet blossoms breathed upon by Love; he carried a mystic veil of saffron colour, which descended from his head upon his shoulders even to the ground, and his shining body was half girt with fawn-skin; in his hand he carried a staff, whose bareness burst forth in almond-bloom, and dancing tongues of flame burnt but did not consumed it; looking upon his face, it appeared as the face of one dwelling in the Holy Place, glowing with the perfect peace which is shed of Love, for he had borne the Very Love within his hand therefore upon him the shadow of the burden of humanity had not rested; and now, encouraged by his gentle mien, and by the strengthened light upon the eyes of my Soul, I went forward until I set myself in front of him who bore the saffron veil; the waves of Love that moved about him laved my face, they refreshed me and appeared to make my self-consciousness sit lightly upon me, and to loosen me from the grip of my humanity, but it was not yet vouchsafed to me to cast it from me. As the man Isaiah prayed to be purged of his transgressions by the burning coal of charity, so I, too, desired that my lips be touched, and my eyes made clear and worthy to behold those things whence flow the springs of life.

When the aspect of him who the bore blossoming staff fell upon me it generated a stronger yearning towards the Beatific Vision, and the distant harmonies of the sphere became clearer unto me; I then first felt conscious that a faint light hovered about my own head, like that upon the head of my Soul, and the voice of him who bore the mystic veil spoke to me by the spirit, and I heard these words, "before thou art worthy to behold Him whom thou hast so long sought in the perfect fullness of His glory, thou must be purged of all grossness, thou must be clothed utterly with change of raiment, and the dead fruit of thy heart and of thy lips must be put away from thee, and when these things shall have been done, yea, even then thou shalt not see His full effulgence with none between it and thee, but through the veil of Sleep shall it be revealed unto thee: follow me;" then chastened by these words, I again bent my head, and my Soul led me forward. He who bore the flame-girt staff floated lightly along his path of flowers, and the glow about his winged feet made their petals to expand. And now in all humility I stood upon the threshold of a glowing temple; the air about it was moved by the breath of Him who dwelt within, its waves were heavy with the odours that came forth of His presence, and its pulses echoed with the voices of the worlds that revolve because of Him. Within the court of the temple I heard the sound of wings that ceased not to beat the air; then a tremor came upon my hands and feet, for remembrance brought to me the image of him we saw by the grey sea, bound hand and foot, and the voice from his heart sounded yet in my ears. Then One came unto me, having six wings, which overshadowed my Soul and me, and though I looked not upon his face, I knew he touched my forehead and lips with it, and they were purified by fire, but not seared with its sting. Then his fellow came unto me, and clothed me with the vestment in colour like the heart of an opal, and over my left shoulder he laid a stole tinted like the inner petals of a white rose, and he placed upon my head a veil which covered my eyes, but did not dim my spiritual vision; and now again the words which came from Love's mouth, when I saw him bound by the sea, rang in my ears, "Thou hast wounded my heart," and a deeper humility fell upon me; then I heard him of the winged feet say unto my Soul, "He is prepared, come" and I was borne along by the spirit through the outer court and toward the Holy Place, and ever the rushing sound of the wings became louder and louder, and I knew that the temple was filled with seraphim, for the veil which hung over my eyes but shielded them from a light, which, when it should fall upon them, would blind; also I knew that he whose head was bound with violets had left us and consigned me to the care of my Soul. Now there arose before the image of him whom we had seen sleeping in the ruined temple; his arms were wound about his head, which lay back upon them; he was naked, but his form was wrapped about with the soft star-lighted air; his lashes were no longer moist with tears, but his face shone as became one though whom the Very Love was to be revealed. And now I felt the heart of the universe beat, and its inner voices were made manifest unto me, the knowledge of the coming presence of the Very Love informed the air, and its waves echoed with the full voices of the revolving spheres, the image of sleep filled the orbit of my sight, and through the veil of his form I saw him who bore the mystic saffron raiment wherewith he had covered his hands. My spirit well-nigh fainting, I turned unto my Soul, and I knew by the increasing glow upon him that strength was given me yet again to lift my eyes. Well was it for me that what came was revealed to me through the veil of Sleep, else I could not have borne to look upon it. From out the uplifted hands of him who stood within the Holy Place there sprang forth a radiance of a degree so dazzling that what else of glory there was within the temple was utterly obscured; as one seeing a thin black vapour resting before the face of the mid-day sun, so I saw upon the radiance the brooding cherubim, their wings meeting, their faces hidden; beyond the crystal within the glory, I saw the Very Love, the Divine Type of Absolute Beauty, primæval and eternal, made of the white flame of youth, burning in ineffable perfection. I could look no longer; in the stream which issued from his heart my spirit was swallowed up, and I knew no more.

TWO TREATISES ON SCIENTIFIC SUBJECTS

With

Nobel and Striking Views of Remarkable Women

By the Author of "The Diving Bell from an Emotional Point of View, and in its Relations to Political Economy", "Lyrics of the Heart", "The Shudders and Other Ailments of the Lower Classes, and How to Treat Them", "Mrs. Gamp as a Symbol of Psychological Progression", "Moral Tales," Etc. Etc. Etc.

Printed from benevolent motives and at the desire of my Aunts Julia and Sarah, but in opposition to the wishes of our old servant, who dislikes printing—because, forsooth, she cannot read.

A TREATISE ON ASTRONOMY

With streaming eyes I gaze upon the stars,
While asteroids urge their hideous course round Mars;
The earth revolves at angles right upon her axis:
The moon in her fifth quarter pallid waxes;
No wonder, some one said, if all were known,
For the equator tilts the torrid zone.
From a long and impressive poem by myself.

I LOVE astronomy; and the idea of its being so neglected as it is pains me: some people cannot bear it. O dear, I can amuse myself for hours with the study; nothing to me is prettier than the stars, Boots and other constellations. Galileo was a creditable astronomer; but he went against the Pope, so I cannot think much of him. Then there was Copernicus (I once spelt his name with K to annoy some one), who found out the brass meridian with a microscope; he was a very good man, but had not sufficient application. Dr. Watts speaks of astronomy in his hymns, notably in that one commencing "Twinkle, twinkle, little star;" but he did not go at all deeply into the subject, although, in but two houses from his own residence, there was a family who possessed a telescope. Life is indeed a riddle. I know a young astronomer, and he prefers meteors to most things in that way, but he also thinks a great deal of comets; but then they give one a world of trouble to find out, even with a theodolite and smoked glass. He found out a plan for tracing their course with a piece of string and some blotting paper, I believe, but I am not sure; it must have been considerable bother.

I think astronomy ought to be more studied, and then more would be known about it, although I must needs confess I have often thought it inquisitive looking at things through glasses, especially so far off. Some people know nothing of astronomy, which is worse than all, they lose so much; but then they study other things, such as botany, geology, and rowing. Galileo could not bear the planet Saturn, I believe, but I would rather not say so before any one, it is because he did not discover it himself; so we see that jealousy exists among astronomers as well as among women. I know a lady that cannot bear her husband to move from her side, because she is so jealous; but the motives that actuate her are different from those of the great astronomer with regard to the planet Saturn. It is, after all, a matter of taste, Jupiter has belts; but then Saturn has a luminous ring round him. I love astronomy because I always think that it keeps young people out of harm's way; but then other things do so too, such, for example, as music, croquet, and logarithms, and I must not omit history. Some shallow people think astronomy stupid, and they give utterance to the following sentiment; "O! it will be all the same in a hundred years;" but that is a poor argument against a study which is harmless surely, if it be nothing else; yet it is sometimes dangerous, for we know a young lady with a mole on her left cheek, who once struck her forehead very violently against a telescope, as she was about to look for some constellation or other, I think it was the Pleiades; that is neither here nor there; but the accident happened as much through her own carelessness as the fault of the science. An opera glass is hardly sufficiently strong for astronomical purposes, and a stethoscope is well-nigh useless; give me a good old-fashioned telescope, with the end to which one applies the eye uncovered, of course; one cannot be too careful, also, to close the eye that is not applied to the instruments and not the eye that is. I remember, when I was once staying with a very well-to-do friend, looking in vain for the North Pole with the eye applied to the telescope closed, but on its being remarked, I rectified the error, and have profited by the criticising of many indeed, any obstructing object, to the other end of it; I lost a great deal of time and experience through this absurd behaviour on the part of a friend, whom I now no longer regard as one. To apply the ear to a telescope is a tempting of Providence; in fine, it is absurd to apply anything but the eye to it. The telescope, rightly used, may prove a great blessing, so also may the microscope, but this is to examine fleas and such things with. I cannot look at a microscope without a feeling of irritation, so to say.

There is, or was, a telescope in the New Road, that must have cost pounds, and yet it is never employed; were it mine, I should sell it, and give the proceeds to the poor, then many a starving family would have cause to bless astronomy: that my instincts are charitable, this last sentiment will show.

I will now proceed to mention some of the things in astronomy that I like best, not that I desire to influence your tastes one way or another: first, the brass meridian; this always interests me a great deal, but I have lost mine lately. The celestial globe is useful, but I must needs confess I think it much overrated: I also have a religious objection to it, on account of the pagan names given to the constellations; but yet it has merit. I have lost mine, and, to say truth, I have neither means nor inclination to purchase another. There are many who use a paper knife to point out the stars with, some use a toothpick or quill, and my aunt knew a lady with grey eyes and a most intelligent cast of countenance who used a hairpin during the winter solstice, and a bodkin, somewhat injured or tarnished, during the summer solstice; but bless you! these, after all, are but comparatively minor points. It is known that Sir J. Herschel covered his globe with brown holland when not using it while others of the opposite school employ green baize hemmed by a trustworthy seamstress. To think that one can become an astronomer by purchasing a globe, a telescope, or microscope is absurd; a man must, in the first place, have a natural gift; and secondly, he must devote portions of his time to studying the science.

I should advise you to procure Sir J. Herschel's book, and to glance over it, and note down at your leisure those passages which strike you particularly with such expressions as the following, "O! Ah! Yes, indeed; to be sure; really; what passion. Ah! I've felt so myself; Humph! (that is for disapproval) and so on. But consult rather your own feelings than my suggestions. The moon is very curious (I say this with all diffidence, but I am not alone), and has two phases, one being called in periwig, the other in apology; a third is gibbous (but that is an epithet which certainly I care little to apply to the moon; let us leave it to those who do). I cannot tell one phase from another, but the first is the most popular. Then there is the harvest moon, but not much, and half moon, of which there is less. The full moon is when it is quite fine and dry.

The moon revolves round the earth at right angles, and describes a circle at great length. I do not consider (but remember I speak from individual feeling) the earth to be included in astronomy, as it is not found in the celestial globe. This, however, would apply to the other planets, only more so. (I say "only more so" in extenuation; if any exception be taken to the expression, let it be considered unsaid.)

The moon affects the tides in the following remarkable manner; but of this more anon. Astronomers employ every means in their power to perfect themselves in their science, but I dare boldly assert that they will make little progress while they use the present calendar. The sun is the most luminous of the heavenly bodies, and gives light to the earth during the season in great quantities. Anyone so minded can find out the altitude of the sun with a spectroscope (the matting being removed, of course) and a little patience; but I always carry a watch. The sun gives its name to several public-houses, but this is by no means its only merit or use; it has many others, which will appear in due order and sequence.

For my part (I may be singular, but so it is), I like the asterisks, they are so very pretty. You can find them out in the heavens with a looking-glass or gyroscope, and on the celestial globe with the naked eye. There are several asterisks all more or less so. (I do not say that in an invidious sense; I simply state a fact.)

I can't bear the milky way, but that may be mere prejudice and a too careful training in one direction; I never could find it out, but that I attribute, in no slight measure, to a large piece of orange peel and some nutshells having got into the telescope. Of course I do not disbelieve in its existence, but I have as yet seen neither use nor beauty in it. (This may be considered undue warmth, but I am one of an impulsive family.) You can see most of the planets when the telescopes act properly, but dear me! odd as you may think it (my aunt's the same), I seldom employ them, now I live out of town, but use smoked glass, more especially for eclipses. I have an authority in Mr. Norman Lockyer, who had a whole drawing-room window carefully smoked for himself and friends, not, you must understand me, that eclipses are planets; you do not take me for a poor fool. I was invited to attend the eclipse expedition, but our old servant declaring that it boded the end of the world, I remained at home. An eclipse is caused by the earth passing through the sun in the month of July, but this could never happen were the brass meridian in working order. An eclipse would frighten one out of one's wits, if one knew nothing of science and had a clouded conscience. Our old servant shuts herself up in a cupboard during an eclipse, and, did I not understand astronomy, believe me I should do the same. (My aunt says it is pardonable weakness; I say nothing.) I do not think much of perihelions and the like. I had some in a bottle, but I confess I did not think them very amusing: they are connected in some way with the sun. An eclipse of the moon is very curious. (I do not lightly say this, I have authority and precedent, so let it not be misconstrued.) I saw a very wonderful one in a kaleidoscope at an astronomical friend's. He described the phenomena to me admirably while a young lady and gentleman played appropriate airs on the guitar and bassoon; a kaleidoscope is the same, fundamentally and subjectively, as a telescope, but bless you! very much prettier. Mr. Lockyer uses one covered with gold paper, but humbler aspirants are content with plainer instruments. (For my part I hold my peace, one bad thing in this world, as my aunt would say.) The patterns were very beautiful pro-duced by the fallen fragments of the moon during its progress through the earth.

In the dark ages the ignorant imagined the earth to have been square, but the discovery of America, the invention of printing, and the Reformation tended to disprove this. Tycho, Brahe and Galileo, whom I

have already mentioned (and I have also honourably
mentioned Copernicus—I desire to give credit where
credit is due), were both eminent and good men, but
as they arranged the fixed stars alphabetically they
denied the existence of more than twenty-six; they
were neither strict Catholics. Give me Copernicus,
bless you! he was the best; a fine, honest-hearted,
open-handed fellow as ever stepped, with an ear ever
open to the wail of the widow and the owl of the
orphan (observe the striking alliteration in the last
sentence; it was a sudden inspiration, with no undue
sacrifice of sense to sound), nevertheless, he placed the
earth among the planets, and rarely, if ever, employed
smoked or even stained glass in the matter of eclipses.
(I believe I mentioned that on one occasion I spelt his
name with a K; it was to gratify a grudge against one
who had done me a considerable injury.)

The three planets, Georgium Sidus, Uranus, and
Herschel are visible to the naked eye in engravings and
diagrams, but not in the heavens save with the help of
a powerful horoscope, unstrapped, of course; but that
always makes such a mess. I will now speak of the
earth, although not belonging so much to astronomy
as physic. It is next to Venus, and its orbit is an irregular parabolic parallelopiped, varying, however, with
the wind; its orbit is very considerable, and estimated
at •00002, old style, but this is considerably regulated
by the weather. In summer it gets hot and expands,
in winter cold and contracts. (This I remember from
a most distressing circumstance, which you would

not easily induce me to allude to.) Nice is the nicest place to winter in. (Observe the pun I cut in the last sentence.) Some say that the earth is flattened at the poles, but for my part (I may be old-fashioned) I can neither bear to say nor to hear prejudicial things said; and I warrant you, if I chose to take up my parable, I could say a great deal more about the earth, such as the equator, latitude, mean temperature, colonial produce and shops; but things are so misconstrued, and so much is made out of so little, that it is better to hold one's peace. And there I will say and maintain that my aunt, hot-headed as she is, is quite right, and where she's right I will give her right.

The tides are astronomical; the spring tides are caused by the sudden application of the brass meridian to the surface of the globe, and the neap tides can only (mark) take place when the moon is on the sea, that is, when there is no eclipse, and the earth's tangent is three quarters projected upon it. (This is only to be understood relatively, as the tides, under such circumstances, are confluent or refluent.)

The hour-glass is very useful in astronomy for the regulation and minute calculation of falling stars and aeronauts; our old servant, whom I have already mentioned, also employs one during the boiling of eggs. Waterspouts are seen in the Yellow Sea; they are very destructive. I have seen a water-spout—I shall never forget it—it took off the water from the sink in our old servant's scullery. The typhoon is also very fearful; it is not uncommonly seen in Japan, and is caused by the rapid revolutions of the brass meridian when the globe is out of order, owing, not infrequently, to the tiresome habits of children. It is almost useless to attempt to study astronomy while your aunt (it matters not how right-minded she be) jogs your elbow. (This is an actual experience.)

**THE END
OF THE TREATISE ON ASTRONOMY**
(*unfortunately*).

A TREATISE ON CHEMISTRY

The cultivation of a science not only tends to elevate our hearts and enlarge our heads, but it strengthens us in filling any position to which we are destined; nay, it is even more than all this, but you will with difficulty persuade me to define what that more is.—*Extract from a lengthy and attractive work by myself*

WITHOUT some slight knowledge of chemistry we make but a sorry figure in society. The electrifying machine now has a place at the fireside of the poor man as well as that of the rich, and the air-pump is enshrined in the hearts of thousands; chloride of lime and magnate of silesium are excellent substitutes for butter at breakfast; and no mother whose heart yearns towards her offspring should be without a hydraulic battery; the stomach-pump is indissolubly mixed up with our tenderest sympathies; and who, O! who is there with so little soul as not to feel the stirring influences of the Leyden jar?

Well has the prophet said, "Man wants but little here below, nor wants that little long."

The experiments that can be made in Chemistry are various, but not infrequently dangerous and un-successful; in the interests of humanity I would rather they should be the latter than the former. My mother, a person of determination, never would allow me to make experiments in the upper part of the house, nor would our old servant (mention of whom you may possibly remember, not, however, under the name of her second husband, Bunkin) permit them in the kitchen; so that my knowledge is limited by reason of these prohibitions. One may make beautiful experiments with the sewing machine, but there is always danger attending them if the instrument be not well supplied with material. The magnet is very interesting: I have not infrequently raised a needle some inches from the table by its aid; I once drew a little girl who had been under a course of steel medicine some feet towards me with a magnet and a fig. Our old servant (alluded to above) said she believed it was the fig which attracted it; but people in her position, it little imports how well-meaning, know nothing of these matters. The compass is both interesting and useful to a certain degree, but it has ever seemed to me a grave disadvantage that it points only to the north (and I may say that in this I do not stand alone). I have a pair of compasses, but they belong rather to mathematics than chemistry. I can amuse myself for hours with an electrifying machine; but, bless you! I cannot abide to touch one. The first time I saw one

I cut such a poor figure, for I expected that it would play tunes when the handle was turned, and I frankly expressed my surprise at its not doing so. (I do not regret admitting this; my aunt said that at my age she was the same.) I remember that there is a handle to them, but it is really so long since I have seen one that I almost forget. The method of testing one of these machines is to form one of a ring round it, and so to receive the shock. Our old servant said she thought it was wicked, as sparks flew out, but she succumbs to superstition, although she is very kind and faithful. She cannot bear chemistry, nor indeed any kind of science, little knowing that even in the boiling of a kettle is involved no inconsiderable principle of science. Steam is a wonderful thing, and Dr. Watts was one of its most skilful exponents; a great deal will yet be done with steam, but not by sitting with one's hands before one. I once had a most interesting interview with a very eminent chemist, now no more, as my aunt would say (I allude to my aunt Julia; my aunt Sarah has but little sentiment); he had arranged in his laboratory, or, as he sometimes playfully called it, shop, many strange and engrossing things, such as tooth powder, hair grease, infants' india rubber rings, ipecacuanha lozenges, and rose drops. These last interesting things were the means of expanding my mind scientifically through the co-operation of sensation. I was induced to essay the following experiment with one, nay, more than one: I placed them on my tongue, and by employing suction I absorbed them into my system; thus may we turn to an intellectual account such simple circumstances. I have just received a bill of considerable length from the successor of this chemist, and I have, at the instigation of my aunt (my aunt Sarah, I should particularise), been induced to dispute his right to charge as exorbitantly as he has done for some things.

The electric telegraph is a continual source of amusement and pleasure to me; the means by which it is worked is very simple: the electrifying machine is placed in the office, and the shock is communicated to the clerk, who loses no time in pulling the wire and pronouncing at once the required letter. It not only betrays a want of taste to interrupt him when thus occupied, but such a course might be productive of serious results. Here handles are employed sometimes of common deal and sometimes of mahogany. Our old servant (who is not wholly unknown to my readers, and whose name was formerly Shum) says she would rather be in her shroud than employ one of these, I cannot but feel, useful instruments; but her views on this, as on other subjects, are undoubtedly narrow. The telegraph was invented by the late Prince Consort during leisure moments at Windsor Castle. At first it did not meet with general approval on account of its rationalistic tendencies, and the affair was hushed up for a time; but Her Majesty subsequently caused a power of attorney to be stamped at a court-martial convened for the express purpose, and it is now in general use. The quantity of wire requisite is a great expense. (My aunt said this; the acumen of the remark will be apparent to all capacities.) In rough weather much damage is done to the telegraph wires;

this would probably account for the bad spelling of the communications. In some houses there are set up telegraphs for the amusement of the members of the family, and it would have afforded us at once gratification and instruction to have had one at home; but our old servant (a person of unaccountable caprice, although trustworthy of untold gold) said she would not stop another hour in the house if it was turned into a heathen orgy; and, as she had been in the family forty years, the plan was abandoned. Thus, alas! it is with everything; she cries and sulks for days if the slightest proposal is suggested in the house out of the common way.

One can make beautiful experiments with soda water and an infusion of brandy. It is asserted that Leibnitz employed sherry; but the essential principle is the same. I know of few things more satisfactory than this. We had an exhausted receiver in the lumber-room, but as our old servant declared the room was haunted, we were not permitted to put this interesting instrument to any use. I remonstrated about this both with her and my connections, but the former cried so bitterly, and stated so repeatedly that she was sick and tired of it, that she was, and hinted in a sinister manner that St. Pancridge was her parish, that I was glad to let the matter rest for a space. I once attended a highly interesting course of lectures with experiments at the Royal Institution; indeed I cannot value sufficiently the instruction afforded me on those occasions. Professor Faraday was the lecturer, a name known to us all; the scene was one of thrilling

excitement: the hall was full of vapour of an overpow-
ering and disagreeable character. The arrangements
were as follows: the lecturer was flanked on his right
by an electrifying machine, while he was supported
on his left by an air-pump and a receiver, very much
exhausted: various preparations were placed before
him on a table kept at the Institution for these honourable purposes, but when not required is put into
another and less important room. One of the lectures
was on ozone and its various influences. Soon after
the lecture was commenced, a feeling crept over me
such as one feels after extinguishing the taper at one's
bedside. That the lecture had no little merit I was fully
convinced, for I was frequently roused from this condition by the clapping of hands, the sharp blows of
umbrellas against the floor, cat-calls, &c.

Another of the lectures was on the steam-engine in
connection with the power-loom, and their influences
on civilisation and modern thought; but I suffered at
the time from so acute a tooth-ache, that I failed to
appreciate this as highly as other discourses. However,
these subjects cannot but interest us deeply.

The screw in naval affairs is very engrossing and
strangely fascinating, and is a vast improvement on
the old system: One seldom sees a sailor without his
screw, nor, indeed, a ship without its crew. (Remark
the two-fold pun in the last sentence; one should leave
no means untried by which to instruct.) The screw
is tied on to the stern of the vessel, and propels it by
means of steam. An honest Jack Tar had his leg injured
by one some time since; he now sits at the corner of

Regent Street, with a picture that has considerable merit, painted by himself, and representing in vivid colours and an original style the unfortunate circumstance. He has a very intelligent face. I frequently stop and question him regarding the accident and other matters, rattling at the same time a few halfpence in my pockets, one of which I have often thought of bestowing upon the poor, honest fellow.

Nothing pleases me more than machinery. A visit to any manufactory has a strange charm to me, especially when accompanied by a sympathetic and congenial companion.

One should be careful never to touch the straps which pass from one wheel to another.

Our old servant (whom you will possibly remember my speaking of on a former occasion) had a grandson whose ear was taken off by a machine, so she is not a little bitter about such things. I have heard her observe she would as lief be in heaven as in a factory; but, although inexpressibly faithful and attached to our family, yet she usually fails to see more than one side to any question.

We knew a poor lad struck blind through some steel points being sent into his eyes while working at a soap boiler's. He was the only prop and support of an old aunt, who has recently been induced to accept the honourable office of pew opener at St. Pancras Church. I may further say, that she is on visiting terms with our old servant. Indeed, through this circumstance we learned the accident sustained by her nephew. My connections inform me that she is a great

gossip, but, it is thought, very well meaning. She has
been heard to say that her nephew's eyes "is a regler
pleg to her."

My Aunt Julia has a domestic who formerly kept
company with a respectable young man who suffered
from an affection of one eye, but it did not inconven-
ience him in his calling—that of a die sinker. He saw
perfectly with the remaining eye. Permit me to relate
yet one more circumstance of a kindred nature. Our
old servant has, at odd times, to help her in the servants' hall and adjacent offices, a girl who suffers peri-
odically from soft knee, from working at percussion
cap making. I have not mentioned these things for the
mere sake of parading our social position, but rather
to bring before your notice sacrifices that have been
made in the noble cause of science, holocausts offered
up at the shrine of modern progress and civilisation.

We have made great strides in chemistry during
the last few years, but we have much more to do yet;
but we shall fail to accomplish the utmost if we do not
put our shoulders to the wheel, and, as the Orientals
say, "'Tis the last straw that breaks the camel's back."

I was formerly much attached to a young cousin,
who made a most curious and ingenious gig out of
cardboard, and painted it a vivid black. He had a
distinctly mechanical turn, and he could, strange to
say, amuse himself for hours with a stomach-pump.
We were great friends, he and I; he had a sweet dis-
position, but a painful stutter. On one occasion his
father—yes, if my memory fails me not, it was his
father—bought him a hand-book of chemistry, which

his servant, quite unjustifiably, as it seems to me, put behind the chimney-back; the right place, she said, for such like trumpery. She had been in their family, an old Bayswater family, for more than thirty years, and, as a domestic, bore an unimpeachable character, marred by a too inflexible will in wrong directions.

THE END (*more's the pity*) OF
THE TREATISE ON CHEMISTRY.

A VISION OF LOVE REVEALED
IN SLEEP

UPON the waning of the night, at that time when the stars are pale, and when dreams wrap us about more closely, when a brighter radiance is shed upon our spirits, three sayings of the wise King came unto me. These are they:—*I sleep, but my heart waketh*; also, *Many waters cannot quench love*; and again, *Until the day break, and the shadows flee away*; and I fell to musing and thinking much upon them. Then there came upon me a vision, and behold, I walked in a land that I knew not, filled with a strange light I had not seen before; and I was clad as a traveller. In one hand I carried a staff, and I hid the other in the heavy folds of a colourless garment; I went forward with my eyes cast upon the earth, pondering, and dazed as one who sets forth upon a journey, but who knows not yet its goal. Then I besought my spirit to make itself clearer before me, and to show me, as in a glass, what I sought; then knowledge came upon me, and I looked within my spirit, and I saw my yearning visibly manifested, and great desire was born, and sprang forth and strengthened my feet and quickened my steps. Now I stood among olive-trees, whose leaves and boughs lay still upon the air, and no light was cast upon them. Then the deep silence was broken by the stirring of the spirit within me; my frame appeared to be rent, and a faintness fell upon me, and for a little space I knew nothing, so powerfully the spirit wrought within me. Then afterwards, as when one who works miracles lays his healing finger upon another who is maimed, and makes him whole, so was my strength renewed, and I lifted up my eyes; and behold, the form of one stood by me, unclothed, save for a fillet binding his head, whereof the ends lay upon either side his neck; also upon his left shoulder hung a narrow vestment; in his right hand he bore a branch of dark foliage, starred with no blossoms; his face had on it the shadow of glad things unattained, as of one who has long sought but not found, upon whom the burden of humanity lies heavy; his eyes, half shaded by their lashes, gave forth no light.

I knew that my Soul stood by me, and he and I went forth together; and I also knew that the visible images of those things which we know only by name were about to be manifested unto me. When I gazed into the lampless eyes of my Soul, I felt that I saw into the depths of my own spirit, shadow meeting shadow. Then my Soul first spoke, and said unto me, *Thou hast looked upon me, and thou knowest me well, for in me thou but seest thyself, not hidden and obscured by the cruel veil of the flesh. I am come forth of thee for thy well-doing, therefore see to it that thou do me no injury.*

By me shalt thou attain unto the end I know thou seekest, for he whom we go forth to find may only in his fullness be manifested by my aid; for whom he appears to those who, with dimmed eyes, grope in the waking darkness of the world, I am put aside, and he is not fully known. By me alone shalt thou behold him as he absolutely is; but in visions shall he be seen of thee many times before his full light be shed upon thee, and thy spirit shall be chastened and saddened because of them, but is shall not utterly faint. Look upon me, and I will support thee, and in thy need I will bear thee up. Looking upon me thou shalt read thine inmost self, as upon a scroll, and in my aspect shall thy spirit be made clear. Come.

Then we went forth towards a dim sea at ebb, lying under the veil of the mysterious twilight of dawn. On its grey sands sat one whom I knew for Memory. Over her face passed the changeful alternations of sun and cloud, shade and shine; the voice of the shell which she held to her ear unburied the dead cycles of the soul; it sang to her of good and evil things gone by, and her introverted eyes looked upon them as when one looks in a mirror upon all else save oneself. My Soul turned his dusky eyes upon me, and then I too heard the voice of the shell; and the ocean cast up my dead before my eyes, and all was unto me as though it had not gone by. Memory bore upon her head and breast a light rain of faded autumn leaves and blossoms, and upon her raiment small flecks of foam had already dried; her lips trembled with the unuttered voices of the past, but she did not weep.

Then I was carried back in the spirit to the time past, and as I walked forth by my Soul, my gaze was drawn inward, and I beheld myself in one of the sunny places of the world; and there was a mist arising from the joy of nature, and my spirit seemed to dance within me. And I beheld, after a space, that the mist formed itself into many visible objects, which all gave me a delight such as one feels in looking upon the golden circles which play within the depths of a sun-lighted pool; and beyond the mist I discerned the forms of many whom Memory brought back to me; they had no radiance about their heads, but their countenances bore no shadow upon them, and the light in the air wherein they moved made a music which was very pleasant unto me. As the heart sits enthroned within the body, and its pulses inform it, so sat one in their midst whose spirit made their feet to dance and their mouths to sing; she rested beneath the shade of an autumn apple-tree, and the sun had kissed her body as it had kissed the fruit of the tree and made it glow: she was naked, but guile was removed from her, therefore she knew it not: the aspect of her face was as that of the face of a child who hears new things, and holds its breath, lest the one who relates them should make too quick an end; her grey eyes looked forth without fear, and in their soft depths were mirrored the things about her that she loved so well; by her side sported all joyous, simple creatures, and she was of them and one with them; the shadow of the burden of conscious-ness had not fallen upon her; she had not known the sickness of the soul, for within the ark of her body the soul had found no resting-place. Looking upon her, I saw that she was good, but I knew that there was that about her that left me not content; she was even as sweet notes heard once and lost for ever.

Then I withdrew my gaze from my spirit, and raised my eyes and looked upon my Soul, and he spoke these words unto me: *It is well that thou hast thus looked upon Pleasure which is past, for with the greater ardour dost thou now desire him whom we go forth to seek: canst thou hear to look forward?* Then, as we went along, while the shallow wave drew back from the grey beach, my spirit took upon itself a great sadness; and lifting my eyes I beheld one, whom I then knew not, seeking shelter in the cleft of a rock. The shame that had been done him had made dim those thrones of Charity—his eyes; and as the wings of a dove, beaten against a wall, fall weak and frayed, so his wings fell about his perfect body; his locks, matted with the sharp moisture of the sea, hung upon his brow, and the fair garland on his head was broken, and its leaves and blossoms fluttered to the earth in the chill air. He held about him a sombre mantle, in whose folds the fallen autumn leaves had rested: and now he came forth of his sheltering place, and as he went along the light upon his head was blown about in thin flames by the cold breath of the sea; and I saw moving beside him in the grey air the spirits of those who had brought him to this pass, and the sound of their mockings fell upon my ears. Then my spirit sighed very heavily within me, and I could look no longer, for I discerned in that company the image of myself; and then all this vision passed away.

I held my regard upon the earth, and marvelled
at what I had seen; and I communed in sadness with
my spirit, for I then knew the part I had taken to hold
Love in contumely, and how I had been one of those
who plant rue, thinking to behold myrtles spring
therefrom; and my spirit being chastened, I lifted my
eyes to my Soul, and I saw upon his face the pale light
of sorrow; yet I remembered how he spoke to me at
the first, and told me that he would uphold me, and
that my spirit should not faint utterly. Then he and I
went on gradually ascending a sandy slope, patched
here and there with scanty grass; and against the pale
sky we saw one, for whom, looking upon him, my
Soul dissolved in tears, so stricken with unavailing sorrow was he, so wounded beyond the hope of healing,
bound hand and foot, languishing under the weight
of his humanity, crushed with the burden of his so
great tenderness. I looked upon the face of my Soul,
and I knew that he, in whose presence we now stood,
was Love, dethroned and captive, bound and wounded, bereft of the natural light of his presence; his wings
drooping, broken and torn, his hands made fast to
the barren and leafless tree; the myrtles upon his brow
withered and falling; and upon that heart, from whose
living depths should proceed the voice of the revolving
spheres, there was a wound flowing with blood, but
changing into roses of divinest odour as it fell. I stood
motionless, my eyes refusing to look longer upon my
stricken lord, then drawn unto my Soul, from whom
I had no comfort; the voice of the shell of Memory
yet sounded in my ears, and I knew that the divine

captive read my spirit's inmost thoughts; from his lips proceeded inaudibly the words, *Thou hast wounded my heart.*

After a moment of mystical agony, I raised my eyes; and behold, the vision of Love was gone. Yea, and upon my own heart the words of Love became engraven, and ringed it about with flame; and then I knew to the full how my hands had been among those which had bound and wounded Love thus. Albeit my spirit found how unworthy it was to receive the odour of the roses which came forth of his heart, yet it clung about me, and became as it were a crown to my head, and I was even lifted up because of my humiliation. Then I turned unto my Soul, and saw that his gaze was bent upon me with pity, and he spoke these words: *Alas I look well into thy spirit, search thy heart and pluck from it its dead garlands, cast them from thee and make it cleans and prepare it for him who shall hereafter enter therein; thou art even puffed up because the wound thou hast been one of those to deal sends forth divine fragrance; rather lament that thou hast not left whole the temple whence it comes forth: of thee and of thy like is its destruction: let us go upon our way.* Then we set forward, and silence was between us; the burden upon my spirit lay very heavy, and I knew not how to raise my eyes.

And now a sound of great lamentation clove the dull air; it was as the wail the mother lifts up when the last of the fruit of her body is wrested from her; it was as the cry of one whose anguish may know no respite, whose soul is rent and cast abroad; it entered deep into my spirit. Then he who walked by me spake these words: *Canst thou lift thy gaze upon her who comes across the sea, upon her who is ravening like it and is one with it? Look well upon her, for thou shall behold in her one who would dash thee aside from the path which thou hast chosen. Look well unto thy heart, lest her breath dry up its springs. Behold,* Then I looked out to sea, and there came towards us one whose name I knew was Passion, she who had wounded and had sought to slay Love, but who, in her turn, was grievously wounded and tormented in strange, self-devised ways. The glory of her head was changed into the abiding-place of serpents whose malice knew no lull; her wasted beauty preyed upon itself; her face was whitened with pale fires, a hollow image of unappeased desire; her eyes flowed with unavailing tears; in her right hand she bore a self-wrought sword of flame, and in her left the goodly fruits and flowers she held were scorched and withered, and crawled upon by evil things; her feet were bound in inextricable folds; she was borne forth she knew not whither; her breath was as the breath of the hungry sea, and rest shall not be given unto her. And then the gentle voice of Memory spoke to me, and told me how she who was thus tormented had been at the first like unto her whom I saw in the spirit beneath the shade of the apple-tree, lying in the light of peace; and how the sun had also shone upon her, and made her face to shine; but she looked beyond the fair and happy things that were about her, and lusted after she knew not what; and then the pleasant place wherein she abode with her happy fellows was taken from her, and, as one who hungers after what he has wittingly lost unto himself, so she craved and was not satisfied; she set at naught the gracious things that had been given unto her, and became the paramour of Hate; then she went about seeking to woo Love to her evil ends, and she fared to him as one humble and poorly clad; and Love had pity upon her, and bent his ear to her supplications, for he knew her not; but anon her aspect waxed cruel, and fierce, deceitful flames went forth of her eyes, and dreadful things clung about her, and shamed the air that he made holy, and with her fiery breath she well-nigh slew him; and when I looked upon her and knew that she would have slain Love, pity was congealed in my heart. Then the voice of the shell spoke to me by the spirit, and said, *Thou hast no pity on thyself.* And this vision also passed from us.

Then my Soul spoke unto me these words: *It is even so, thou hast no pity on thyself, for thou too hast essayed to slay Love, as it has been shown to thee, thou hast wounded him: let us set forth, and I will show thee a vision of that which may yet be averted.* Then we fared along by the sea, and its hollow breath fell sore upon my spirit: and anon we came upon a crowd who all bore different aspects, and again among these I chose forth one who was myself; some were mocking, and some carried an air of scorn upon them, and others of deceit; some feigned mourning, and others were not moved by what they saw. Then I approached, bent down by a great awe of sorrow; and through my tear-dulled lashes I looked upon him who had been bound and wounded. He lay as one without life; the voice of his heart was dead within him; looking upon his face it seemed as if the end of all had come, and the air about him was laden with lamentations; upon his pallid brow one had thrown a spray of yew, but his body lay untended, and none had clothed him with his last garment; a thin flame rose from his heart and hovered upon it; and the cords wherewith he had been bound to the tree yet confined his hands, his feet, and his shattered wings; the light about his head had gone, and in its place the sea-froth made a crown; they who were gathered about him when we drew near had left him one by one. For myself a burning shame wrapped me round, and I sank upon the earth, and utterly abased my spirit for a space; then I heard the voice of my Soul speaking to me, and I lifted my eyes, and behold, the dolorous vision was gone. And, my heart laden with weeping, I turned unto my Soul, and he said these words unto me: *Did I not tell thee at the first that whilst thou hadst me by thy side, and didst me no injury, thy spirit should not utterly faint; therefore be not cast down at the grievous vision we go forth from beholding, but lay it as a sign upon thy heart; so shall thou be warned in good time. We now bend our steps towards one who is mighty indeed, and it is given to no man to overcome him; yet when thou shall look upon him, thou shall see of how mild an aspect he is, and so thou shall put terror away from thee. Come.*

And we yet went forth by the sea, until we came upon a temple standing alone; the breath from the heart of the sea came up as the litanies of the dead who lay beneath it, and girt it about and fell cold upon my spirit, and well-nigh made the pulses of my life to cease; but my Soul, faithful as when he first bent his eyes upon me by the olive-trees, supported me; and the door of the temple being touched by the branch which he bore, opened of itself, and my spirit yearned for the further and dreadful mystery that was to be shown me. It was well for me that there abode one beside me who would hold me up, or my heart, frozen within my breast, would have refused to support me, fainting as I was. I raised my eyes, whereof the light had gone out in the black air about us, and sought help of my Soul. He bent towards me, and said, *Cast fear from thee. Behold, thou shalt not fail.*

Before us and over us was a shadow as of the darkness before all things were; Hope was removed from the midst of it, and, looking upon it. Despair seemed to be enthroned therein; and the spirit wholly forgot that light had ever sprung forth upon the universe. Again I sought succour of him who stood beside me, and again it was vouchsafed to me: then, essaying to strengthen my eyes, I looked forward, and I beheld, slowly revealing himself in the heart of the thick darkness, one seated upon a dim and awful throne; he was wrapt about with sighs for raiment, and cypress, heavy with the tears of ages, was the crown upon his head; although his face was hidden in his potent hands when first he was manifested to my sight, yet I knew he wept, and his weeping was as the gathered-up lamentations of all time; how sore it fell upon my heart I may not say; and a great pity was begotten within me, which went forth upon my spirit, towards his throne. Anon he lifted his face, and the sadness and mourning which go forth of the hearts of all men seemed transfigured upon it, and I saw that it was overshadowed with the dark mystery of life: it appeared to me as the face of one who dwells for ever without the Holy Place, upon whose brow the highest radiance may never fall. Then I thought upon the words my Soul had spoken to me, before we entered herein, when he told me how mild of aspect was the face I should look upon. For I saw that his mien had in it an exceeding gentleness, as of a creature that desires to caress and to be caressed, but who dares not approach, lest he bring terror with him—as of one who throughout all eternity bears upon him a loveless burden, whereof he may not rid himself: his was the pallor of one who had wrestled with another strong as himself, and had prevailed, but whose own dominion was as gall to him, the knowledge of whose hateful might gnawed his own spirit through and through with an unquenchable fire, whose power was his humiliation, whose strength his weakness. For a moment's space I could not look upon him, for the memories of his prowess crowded within my heart, and surged up in a bitter stream into my eyes. Then I sought the face of my Soul, and I saw upon its darkness the answer to my unuttered question, and I knew that I stood in the presence of him who had done battle with Love, Death, who would love us did he dare, whom we would love did we dare; for, when he folds us about with the chill white raiment, he sets the seal of his love upon us; and, as the bridegroom and the bride stand linked together, overshadowed by the mystic saffron-coloured veil, and one spirit makes them one; so, at that hour when time slips from us, are we wedded to him before whom I stood, and with the sacrament of his kiss he signs us unto himself, and makes us of one flesh with him. Then I lifted my eyes and looked yet again, and I saw that one stood by the throne, who held his finger upon his lip; he bore in one hand a crystal globe wherefrom the eyes of Death were ever averted, for he might not look therein; upon his head there bloomed a lotos flower, and lotos flowers hid his feet; the fathomless silence of the tomb came up and clothed him as with a pall, and he was girdled round with mystery, and mystery was written upon the air about him; his eyes were fixed upon the globe he held, and made dim because of what he saw therein; and the secrets of the tomb came forth and racked his face, and his face sweated with the pallid fires that rose from the dead he looked upon. And now my spirit welled up beseechingly within me, and looked forth of my eyes, and I turned them upon my Soul's face, as if supplicating; and his face was towards mine, and he knew the question that rested upon my lips, and he spoke and said, *Seek not to look upon the globe for thou assuredly knowest it is given to no man to search its depths and live. He who bears it is Eternal Silence. Behold how his face is seared and furrowed with the things he knows, with the secrets that are laid bare to him. Let his name be a sign unto thee.* He ceased to speak, and my spirit was drawn inward, and I pondered upon what he who brooded upon the throne before me had wrought; and I marvelled the more at his might when I had seen how humble of demeanour he was; and these thoughts came upon me:—When he had rent asunder those newly come together and made one, when he had set at nought the bitter desire of years and the late-found joy, did he wear upon his countenance that great sadness, well-nigh sweet? When the shriek of the mother shattered the night, because the sole one left of her withered blossoms had been plucked by him, and she was left as an uprooted plant cast upon the wave, was he then crowned with humility? When I thought upon those who had made the face of her that bare them to shine, and were as the sun's kiss to her, and how he had wrapt them in his chill raiment one by one in her sight, and I looked upon his eyes whence the tears ceased not to flow, my heart failed within me, and my marvelling became too hard for me. Then I turned towards my Soul and sought his gaze; he fixed it upon me, and spoke these words: *I have read thine inmost thoughts, and they are hard indeed. Of the thing whereon thou hast pondered thou canst, of thy nature, know nothing, but only this:—When he, before whom we stand, bends his face over those whose spirits wing them away, he takes upon it the exceeding gentleness thou hast seen, albeit it is not beheld of them who stand by sorrowing; for they have not looked upon his face; therefore they know it not until he lays his finger upon their lips, and touches them with his own. Let us go forth upon our way.* And he led me as who should lead one lately risen from the couch of disease, weak, and before whom the earth seems to spin, and darkness was upon us.

And my Soul said, *Raise thine eyes and behold somewhat which shall gladden them, as it hath gladdened all men before. Let the balm of this vision sink into thy spirit; so shall it make thee whole of the sickness that came upon thee in the house of Death.* I lifted my eyes, and I saw coming towards us what had the appearance of a bird moving softly along the still, grey air. As it approached us, I perceived two presences, one reclining upon the other who gently fanned the air with great wings. And now a deep calm fell upon my spirit, such as one feels when the burden of a sharp trouble is averted, and my Soul and I wept when we saw him who was being thus carried towards us; he lay lightly across the breast of his supporter, cheek reposing against cheek; upon his head were two small fair wings, and round his brow were bound the flowers and buds of poppies; upon his face there shone a distant light of childhood; his parted lips breathed forth peace; the one who bore him smiled upon him, and rejoiced because of his burden. I knew that he who was winged was called Divine Charity, and his charge Sleep.

When we went forth out of the temple wherein abode Death, we came to a strange land stretching far out towards the wan sea, and inland the earth was overgrown with rank weeds; and ever the voice of the shell of Memory sounded in my ears, and the land to right and left of me seemed to image my past years; the comfort which I had had of Sleep departed from me, and when I sought the eyes of my Soul no rays of consolation came forth therefrom, no blossoms of golden light yet starred the dull branch he bore: the shadow of the house of Death lay heavy upon him. Albeit the burden of great bitterness that was shed upon my spirit by him I saw upon the gloomy throne had choked up the springs of my heart, yet within my breast the flame of yearning towards him who should be the end and crown of my journeying burst forth and impelled me onward; and my spirit told me that in a short space I should look upon him, in what guise I knew not. Therefore I turned my questioning eyes upon my Soul, and a light of sadness fell upon me from his face, and he spoke and said these words: *Alas! not yet shall it he vouchsafed unto thee to behold him in his sovereign glory, clad in radiance, but thou shall see him as he has been carried forth whence we last looked upon him with grief dulled eyes, when he was as one be-reft of life. He, whose bliss it was to make his burden Love is a supreme spring of pity, and men laving themselves in the streams that go forth of him, account themselves blessed; the hurt that has been done them passes by; they are made whole, for he slowly, yet surely, heals them; in his arms the broken of spirit are cherished; and when he holds the hearts that are cleft to his breast they are once more bound together.* And I raised my eyes after he had spoken these words, and sought to gather strength to look upon the coining vision. Now again two came towards us, one bearing the other, and treading down the dark growth of weeds that thickened about us. When I saw him who reposed in the other's arms, a trembling seized me, and an awe came upon me—the awe which is begotten of exceeding pity: around his head shone a faint and flickering light, his white and perfect body was flecked here and there with blood, and, as when we saw him by the sea, betrayed, wounded, and helpless. He who supported him was ravaged with the storms of ages; in his eyes there shone a light of infinite memories; in his ears there rang the voices of unnumbered years; his mien had in it the great tenderness of one unconquerable; as a mother encircles with her arms a beloved and sorrowing child, and softly murmurs to him the songs of his infancy, so he pressed his bruised and smitten charge to his breast, comforting him with the universal voice.

And when this vision was fulfilled, the shell of Memory again sang in my ears, and I knew that what had past was the image of somewhat long gone by; and I humbled my spirit when I knew that I had been among those who consign Love to the arms of Time; casting the potent lord upon the earth, and taking no heed of him; leaving the bruises wherewith he had been buffeted to be tended perchance of none. The earth was now covered with poppies, and the air was heavy with their odours, and I would fain have sought Sleep, but that I knew it was forbidden unto me; moreover, it was given me to know by my Soul, through the spirit, that another vision was shortly to be vouchsafed unto me. The air was murmurous with faint sounds borne on the odour of the poppies: these were the echoes of the voices of my past years. I again sought the eyes of him who walked beside me, and, by the pale light of the first stars, I saw reflected in their depths the vague image of something which stamped a calm upon them; yet, as we set forth along that mystic land, our hearts were still burdened with the weariness of sorrow hard to cast away from us. Then, as my Soul turned towards me, I saw, in the shadows that gained strength about us, that a great presence was gathering itself, and, as we gazed upward, our vision rested upon one seated; around her head burned the light of the new-born stars, whose harmony made glad the pulses of the air; from her wide brow went forth a healing balm; in her aspect all men seek their rest and hide them in her shadow. She bore upon her knees one still beautiful, but pallid with woes, riven with wasting troubles, weary and dying; within her heart she hid his passing spirit; the waning golden light about him faded in the gloom of her hair, the falling blossoms of his head lightly strewed her dusky raiment wherewith she wholly enfolded him; he sank beneath her sacramental kiss, and Day was lulled to death in the all-embracing arms of Night.

And now we went forth upon our dimly lighted path, where the red and purple of the poppies faded into sombre grey beneath the faint rays of the lately risen stars, and the depths of the still pools which lay to right and left of us sent up their pale reflections, and ever the utterances of the sea of my life spoke to me by the voice of the shell of Memory: and this night seemed to be a figure of my years gone by. After my spirit had bent itself to the pondering of these things, I turned towards my Soul, and I saw that his eyes were heavy with the sense of what was to come; also my

84

spirit leapt up, for albeit I was yet ignorant of what was to be shown forth, a voice within me told me that it should be of much import; and I bent towards him who was with me and gazed earnestly upon him, as one importunate, and who sought to be prepared and made ready to receive what would be to his great benefit. And my Soul, seeing my urgency, spoke and said, *Look well upon this shortly to befall us and take great heed unto it, for it will be of weight to thee; and it shall be, as it were, the opening of the scroll whereon we may read the rest. He, whom we relax not in seeking, shall again be revealed unto thee; but, alas, again the pulses of thy heart shall fail when thou seest him; and by the lesson of the vision shalt thou learn that thou art yet unready to behold him in his fullness; yea, and this shall not be the last trial put upon thee. Now shall he set forth before thee somewhat of the history of his shame whom we seek, and, how, as one who brushes not away the cobwebs that have gathered themselves together upon the fair sculpture of one divine and has even said Ha, ha, at the spiders busy upon it; so have men laid upon him the darkness of the earth, as a thick veil wherethrough his light shall not come, I cease; the vision will unfold itself clearly in thine eyes.* Then I looked forward, and I saw that we approached what appeared to be a temple in ruin, long forsaken and not remembered; its crumbling marble walls and pillars, worn by time and storms, glimmered dimly beneath the stars; about it lay the decayed fragments of its dead beauty, and its entrances were choked up with poppies and clinging weeds, but to my spiritual vision there appeared a radiance about it that made me know that the light of him whom I sought penetrated the depths of its enduring gloom. Our heads bowed, and in silence we approached the entrance; we put aside the rank growths which sought to hinder our going in, and stood on its grass-grown threshold; then the silence of my heart was broken by its weeping, and a faintness fell upon me when I lifted up my eyes to the vision now revealed to me. Before us was an altar-like monument carved with a legend of old time, whereon the joyful creatures who sported in procession across it were wasting in decay, time-dis-coloured and riven; upon it he lay, whom, when we stood in the presence of Death, we saw borne to earth by Divine Charity; he was wrapped about with the slumber of those upon whom no shadow has fallen, upon his face there lay that far-off light of childhood; the mildness of his half-formed smile drew the spirit unto itself, his lashes were yet moist with late-shed tears, born not of sorrow but of tenderness; looking upon him, our wave-tossed spirits found their haven, and rest fell upon us.

Before I dared to look upon him who was present with Sleep, and whom I have not wearied of seeking, I saw by the spirit that one rose impalpably from the heart of the poppies, and hovered upon them, lapped in his half-shut wings; his eyes were not covered by their lids, yet it seemed as if slumber had fallen upon them; he fixed his mystic gaze upon a crystal globe he held in both his hands, wherein I knew by the spirit he saw pass the dreams of those who sleep beneath the stars; his locks were softly lifted by the air, and his lips trembled with the weight of the myriads of visions he called forth; his bent face was overshadowed by the exceeding sadness of one who knows the thoughts of men. Again I raised my eyes, and I saw her who had lately been revealed to us receiving the passing breath of day; with unrelaxing gaze, and eyes from whose depths comes forth all gentleness, she watched Sleep, her beloved son; and she, to whom all was as an open scroll, wept when she looked upon him whose heart was as the heart of a little child; her dusky locks flowed forth upon the air, and from their shade the stars sent down their beams; her garments were fragrant with the blossoms begotten of Day's death, and hymns proceeded from the silence that was about her; upon her all supporting arms, and hidden in her raiment, she bore those who slept and dreamed, and those who watched; she whispered peace unto those who know it not when she is not; she put away from them the sword, and healed the wounds that gape and bleed when she is not by to close them; she drew the spirit of the mother to her child who dwells in far-off lands, and in her arms the long-separated were brought together; beneath her shadow the lost little one yet again nestled upon her mother's breast; she hid the stricken in her heart, by her the forsaken were taken back to the hearts of the forsakers; she brooded over the uncared-for with the soft care of her wings, and by her the forgotten were brought to remembrance.

Then I sought my Soul in trembling, for I knew that there was one present on whom I had not yet dared to look, and my Soul said to me by the spirit,

Behold him whom we seek but we are not yet prepared.
Then I turned my gaze upon him; in the gloom of the
unremembered temple he sat in all lowliness upon the
fragment of a broken frieze, whereon the sculptured
histories of his ancient glory crumbled and fell away,
forgotten and uncared for, blighted by the breath of
ages, stained with the rust of storms that know no
mercy; his red and golden raiment hung loose about
his limbs, and the blossoms from his hair had fallen
crisped and dead upon his shoulders; the tears of a divine agony yet lay upon his cheek; the radiance which
I had seen by my spirit, before my feet had gained the
threshold of the temple, sprang from the wound upon
his heart; and when I looked upon and saw it illumine
the dim eyes of my Soul, my spirit abased itself, and
my gaze fell upon the earth. Then I knew that this vision had been fulfilled, and my heart, ringing with the
inner voices of the things that had been revealed to us,
and my eyes laden with their images, I again turned
unto my Soul, and saw that upon his countenance
rested the light that came forth of Love's wound, and
made it shine; and, as we departed from the temple,
I rejoiced secretly at this; also I felt strengthened and
gladdened at heart because of Sleep; and my spirit was
softened by reason of his smile. And we turned our
steps towards the waning stars.

And the awe which comes upon man at the passing away of night fell upon us, and I bethought me
again of the words of the wise king, *Until the day break
and the shadows flee away.* And a strong yearning was
begotten within me, and a sob burst forth from my

mouth up out of my heart, and my lips said inaudibly, *Ah, that the day would break, and the shadows verily and indeed flee away;* and the spirit essayed to escape, and in travail I sought help of my Soul, and it was given unto me, and he spoke these words: *Put thy sorrowing away from thee, for the sword shall not again cruelly cleave thy spirit; yet, as I told thee before we stood upon the threshold of the ruined temple we have erewhile left, another trial shall be laid upon thee, and the spirit must needs crouch beneath the weight of it; but, albeit sorrow shall go up as a mist before thee, when thou beholdest what is at hand thou shalt see, as behind a thick cloud, the presence of light; in the coming vision shall be dimly heralded his effulgence; it shall appear in thine eyes as it were the strong weeping that goes before joy; and as the springing forth of hope from despair: it shall not be seen of thee as a dark mystery; thy spirit will look into it and know it.* He made an end of speaking, and by the pale beams of the sinking stars I saw an image dimly mirrored in his eyes. I removed my gaze from his face, and looked abroad, and beheld, dark against the wan air of the dying night, Love seated upon a throne lowly and poor, and not worthy to bear him,—no longer, indeed, wounded and bleeding, but still bereft of his perfect glory; in his eyes there shone a soft light of suffering not yet past, but on his brow, where poppies were mingled with the myrtles, there lay the shadow which falls upon one not remembered; upon his parted lips hovered the half-formed smile of a child who halts between weeping and laughter; he was fully clothed in raiment of dim and sullied red and gold; in one hand he bore a poppy branch bound about the myrtle, from which the stars had fallen one by one, and in the other a golden globe whose brightness was obscured and shamed by dust; his feet were wholly hidden in the thick growth of weeds and poppies that crowded round his throne; he spoke no word, only the faint sounds in the air about him and the grief-dimmed eyes of my Soul told me that he was Love imprisoned in an alien land of oblivion—forgotten, put away.

Again my heart sank, and the flowing of its streams waxed dull, and the words of him bound by the sea burned upon it with a more ardent flame, and the vision we passed from filled my eyes, and came forth of them in bitter tears; yet I forgot not the saying of my Soul, that this should be as the darkly revealed sign of the joy to come, for was not Love enthroned—poorly indeed—and had not the shadow of suffering wellnigh lifted, albeit indeed its sear remained? But I called up strength, and bound it as a girdle about me, and looked upon the countenance of him beside me; and behold, upon it, despite the eyelids drooping with foregone grief, I saw the longed-for smile, and I took content upon me.

Our course now lay along an upward slope, whereon the poppies waxed scantier, and the weeds less rank; a soft mossy grass soothed our wayworn feet, and I could see by the light of the dying stars that small golden blossoms lay in a pattern upon the sward. As we neared the brow of the hill, I knew that a yet unseen and mysterious presence was about to be revealed to us; soft breezes bore his light to us upon their wings, and voices from the passing Night spoke to us of him; he was half-seated, half-lying, upon a height beyond which was stretched out the faintly glimmering sea; there lay upon him yet the shadow of the Night, but his face had upon it the radiance of an expected glory, the light of glad things to come; his eyes were yet soft with the balm of Sleep, but his lips were parted with desire; his breath was as that of blossoms that awake and lift up their heads and give forth their odours; his dusky limbs were drawn up as if in readiness to depart, and his great and goodly wings softly beat the air; with one hand he cast away his dim and dewy mantle from him, and with the other he put aside the poppies that had clustered thickly about him; as he turned his head to the East, the poppies fell from his hair, and the light rested upon his face; the smile it kindled made the East to glow, and Dawn spread forth his wings to meet the new-born Day. And when the Day was seated on his throne, we passed along a pleasant land that lay beneath the light of a great content; and the radiance yet lingered on the countenance of my Soul, and the sadness that had made the curves of his mouth heavy, and had dimmed his eye, now gradually departed, and there came upon him an aspect of calm, as of one certain of a good thing shortly to befall, although he knows not fully what it may be; and when I looked upon his eyes my spirit took heart, and I girded myself and set forward with my head no more bent; and we were met by many who had been shown me in my former dreams, and who all bore the reflection of a light upon their faces.

Also I saw with great joy many whom I knew by name, and who were dear to me, and they were clad in garments of beauty, so that it joyed my eyes to behold them. And it appeared to me as though I felt beating upon my breast the warmth that came from theirs towards me; and youth was set as a crown upon their heads, and they bore branches blossoming from the breath of youth, and its divine essence coloured all the air about them; and I discerned one face in that company beloved of me beyond the rest; a northern sun had set a ruddy sweetness upon it, and southern suns had kissed it into perfect bloom; from the depths of the grey eyes welled up and sprang forth the spirit of Love, and, most loath to depart, yet brooded upon them as the dove in early time upon the waters; a sacred light, as of the guileless dreams of childhood, looked out from them and gladdened my own, and the softness of Sleep was bound upon the head. When I looked upon the face, I felt, indeed, that my travail was well-nigh over, and as it passed from me, and was lost to me, my spirit bathed its dusty wings in the warm, glad tears that bubbled from my heart, and was refreshed. And when the throne of day was set wellnigh above our heads, and there was that in the air which moves the heart of nature, we rested ourselves beside a running stream, whose waters brought joyous sounds from afar, as it were the long-forgotten songs and gentle voices of our childhood, yet laden with a heavier and fuller harmony from a source we knew not yet; and as we journeyed on in the dawn of the evening, an awe fell upon me, as when one enters upon a new and unknown way, and all the air about teemed with the echoes of things past and the vague intimations of things to come.

Then my Soul turned towards me and spoke these words: *Lay upon thy spirit a glad humility, and essay to strengthen thine eyes, that they may bear to behold the things which shall shortly be brought before thee to thy comfort and solace. As thou hast hitherto only seen him we seek sinking beneath the burdens that have been laid upon him by thee and by the like of thee; as thou hast seen the glory about him shattered and made dull by reason of the wounds and weakness the bitter darkness of the world has inflicted, so shalt thou now behold him gathering his natural power about him, and clothed with light; but not yet shall it be given to thee to see him in the plenitude of his glory. I will support thee. Look up.* And now I raised my eyes and looked upon the stream, and it seemed to me as though the waters were cleft apart, and there was a hollow in their midst; and lo, the air about it appeared changed, and its pulses stood still, and the sounds I had heard borne on its wave collected themselves together and took form; and the form was of the colour of the sun-lighted sea, and within it I saw one borne gently upward, naked, and glowing exceedingly; the stars of the living myrtles burned fresh upon his hair, and his countenance was as the supreme excellence of youth transfigured, the wound upon his heart was healed, and on its place I saw burning a ruddy flame, whereof the tongues came forth to me and touched my own, whereon were engraven the words which I heard Love speak when we saw him bound to the tree, and in their stead the flame wrought this saying, letter by letter, *Many waters cannot quench Love, neither can the floods drown it*; and now the radiant mist wherein he was lifted up rose and enfolded him, and hid his aspect from me, and its form was dispersed, and it was changed to gentle sounds in the stream, and all the air about became as it was before.

Then I turned my eyes upon my Soul and saw that he appeared well pleased, and the sparkling light sent up from the ripples of the stream whereby we sat played across his brow and illumined his dusky hair. Then I knew that I should be gladdened by what he was going to tell me. He spoke and said, *Thou hast well seen that the travail of Love is past and gone by and content and joy are spread over the whole air because of it. Now there will arise upon thy vision a mystery which thou wilt, of thy nature, comprehend but dimly; yet fail not to look well upon it, for by it the springs of the heart of the universe are fed and made glad; and because Love is thus gone up from the wave in thy sight, it is given to thee to look upon it.*

He ceased to speak, and I turned my gaze in the direction where I had seen the last vision; and behold, again the air seemed changed, and I saw a happy light gathering itself there, and it seemed, as it were, to be formed of the warmth which makes the earth bring forth its fruit; and there appeared to me within the light an inner living glow, and the glow divided itself in twain, and became two Holy Ones, each having six wings; their limbs moved not, but the ardour wherewith their spirits were endued bore them along.

As one sees in a soft air two flower-laden branches bend one towards the other, and, mingling, send forth a two-fold fragrance, so I saw one of these impelled towards his fellow and lightly touch him, and a living pulse seemed to beat in the flame that went forth from them, and a form was given to it, and a heart informed it, and all the fire coloured air about it breathed hymns at this marvellous birth. Albeit, my spirit had not yet been fully purified, so that I should clearly know what this mystery showed forth; yet I was greatly rejoiced in that it was given me to see it. And now my Soul turned towards me and spoke these words, *What thou hast just beheld it is vouchsafed to no man to comprehend save he see the glory that comes forth of the Holy Place; therefore gird up thy spirit that thou be ready for the call of him who shall lead thee thereunto. What thou hast seen it was given to the three Holy Ones to know fully when they were cast into the furnace; for as the serpent-rod which the prophet threw forth swallowed its fellows, the greater eating the lesser, so did the fiercer flames of that Charity which thou hast erewhile seen wonderfully and mystically begotten go forth of the righteous children's hearts, and devour and utterly dry up the heat that burned about them.*

He ceased to speak, and then I turned my gaze upon his eyes, and rejoiced greatly through my spirit to see a brighter glow upon them, as from the expected coming of the long-desired; and when I cast my eyes upon the earth I discerned there many happy creatures, joyous and beautiful, and such as have no existence in the neighbourhood of evil. After a space, and when my eyes had been gladdened by reason of these things, I again turned them upon my Soul, and I knew that what we sought would now short-ly be revealed to us. A weakness fell upon me, but my Soul supported me; we looked forward, and saw one approaching clothed about with a soft light; he moved towards us, gently lifted by the spirit from the ground, neither flying nor running. Ever and again his feet, wherefrom sprang glowing wings, touched the earth and caused it to bring forth flowers; his head was bound with a fillet of violet, and violet blossoms breathed upon by Love; he carried a mystic veil of saf-fron colour, which descended from his head upon his shoulders even to the ground, and his shining body was half girt with fawn-skin; in his hand he carried a staff, which was as the rod of the high priest, for as I looked upon it its barrenness burst forth in almond bloom; and, as when the prophet put away his shoes from off his feet before the Holy Place, and beheld the bush burning with fire but not consumed, even so I saw upon the staff the dancing tongues of flame cling round the wood, but leave it scatheless; and this thing appeared marvellous in my eyes, and I thought upon the words my Soul had spoken to me concerning the three Holy Ones, and how the fires which wrapped them about did but make them stronger and fairer than before.

And now, looking upon the face of him who came towards us, it appeared as the face of one dwelling in the Holy Place, glowing with the perfect peace which is shed of Love, for he had borne the Very Love within his hands, therefore upon him the shadow of the burden of humanity had not rested; and now, encouraged by his gentle mien, and by the strengthened light upon the eyes of my Soul, I went forward until I set myself in front of him who bore the saffron veil; the waves of Love that moved about him laved my face, they refreshed me, and appeared to make my self-consciousness sit lightly upon me, and to loosen me from the grip of my humanity, but it was not yet vouchsafed to me to cast it from me. As the holy seer prayed to be purged of his transgressions by the burning coal of Charity, so I too desired that my lips should be touched, and my eyes made dear and worthy to behold those things whence flow the springs of life. When the aspect of him who bore the blossoming staff fell full upon me it generated a stronger yearning towards the Beatific Vision, and the distant harmonies of the spheres became clearer unto me; I then first felt conscious that a faint light hovered about my own head, like that upon the head of my Soul, and the voice of him who bore the mystic veil spoke to me by the spirit, and I heard these words, *Before thou art worthy to behold Him whom thou hast so long sought in the perfect fullness of His glory, thou must be purged of all grossness, thou must be clothed utterly with change of raiment and the dead fruit of thy heart and of thy lips must be put away from thee; and when these things shall have been done, yea, even then thou shall not see His full effulgence with none between it and thee, but through the veil of Sleep shall it be revealed unto thee. Follow me.* Then, chastened by these words, I again bent my head, and my Soul led me forward.

Then I turned unto him and bent a look upon him as of one questioning, and, seeing my aspect, he turned towards me and spoke these words: *Wouldst thou learn who is this thus leading us on towards Him we seek; thou sawest his name upon his brow, but the lingering darkness of thy spirit forbade thee to decipher it aright; he it is whom thou hast known since first thou camest away from thy mother's breast, for with what thou receivedst therefrom, thou acceptedst him; looking upon him thou lookest upon what has ever dwelt within thy heart of hearts, for by him shall the Very Love he revealed unto thee; he has no beginnings for throughout all ages has he stood by and ministered to Him we seek and shown Him forth: it has been desired of many from the first years unto this day to put him aside and even to slay him, but, like the flame-girt, unconsumed staff he bears, he passes through the fire, and even in these latter days gives forth the light that has first been shed upon him. The violets upon his brow are those of young time, yet the dew is fresh upon them; and though it was believed of many that his staff was sapless and withered, behold how the air about it is made fragrant by the blossoms that it bears. Faithful is he through all; he holds on high his lamp so that those who look above the low fogs that cling about the earth may be led of it, and the flames about him penetrate the thick darkness of the waking world. Many have sought to tear the wings from off his feet that they may not see the light that springs forth from them; yet still the radiance of Him whom he shows forth makes his feet shed light abroad, and still the earth yields flowers at his approach. Let us follow him.*

He who bore the flame-girt staff floated lightly along his path of flowers, and the glow about his winged feet made their petals to expand. And now in all humility I stood upon the threshold of a glowing temple; the air about it was moved by the breath of Him who dwelt within, its waves were heavy with the odours that came forth of His presence, and its pulses echoed with the voices of the worlds that revolve because of Him. Within the court of the temple I heard the sound of wings that ceased not to beat the air; then a tremor came upon my hands and feet, for remembrance brought to me the image of him we saw by the grey sea, bound hand and foot, and the voice from his heart sounded yet in my ears. Then one came unto me, having six wings, which overshadowed my Soul and me, and, though I looked not upon his face, I knew he touched my forehead and lips with it, and they were purified by fire, but not seared with its sting. Then his fellow came unto me, and put away my traveller's garb from off me, and clothed me with a vestment in colour like the heart of an opal, and over my left shoulder he laid a stole tinted like a flame seen through water, and he placed upon my head a veil which covered my eyes, but did not dim my spiritual vision; and now again the words which came from Love's mouth, when I saw him bound by the sea, rang in my ears, *Thou hast wounded my heart*, and a deeper humility fell upon me. Then I heard him of the winged feet say unto my Soul, *He is prepared, come*; and I was borne along by the spirit through the outer court and toward the Holy Place, and ever the rushing sound of the wings became loader and louder, and I knew that the temple was filled with seraphim, for the veil which hung over my eyes but shielded them from a light which, when it should fall upon them, would blind them; also I knew that he whose head was bound with violets had left us, and consigned me to the care of my Soul.

Now there arose before me the image of him whom we had seen sleeping in the ruined temple; his arms were wound about his head, which lay back upon them; he was naked, but his form was wrapped about with the soft star-lighted air; his lashes were no longer moist with tears, but his face shone as became one through whom the Very Love was to be revealed. And now I felt the heart of the universe beat, and its inner voices were made manifest unto me, the knowledge of the coming presence of the Very Love informed the air, and its waves echoed with the full voices of the revolving spheres. Then my Soul spoke to me and said, *In the beginning of time the universe and all that was therein was grey, and its springs were without life, as a fair body, joyless and lacking beauty, because no spirit stirs it; light had not come upon it; and, as when one is in a trance, the pulses are dead, and await the aid of that which shall enter them and make the dead alive; even so, there sprang forth, of its own power and holy ardour, a light over the face of all things, and the heat of it made them glow, and the grey became green: the golden air sang over all, and an universal hymn arose and went up, and its voice yet gladdens the circling worlds. As the prophet saw in the dark valley the dead bones come together and take life upon them, even so Love, who was the light, smiled upon the uninformed countenance of things, and it was kindled because of it; and there went from him a two-fold essence, whereof the streams have flowed for ever, and cease not to flow; and by them are we upheld, and our spirits replenished; and, as the priest holds the flow-er-starred crown over the heads of the bridegroom and the bride, so now and again do the streams unite within us, and Love, whence they go forth, is the crown over us and the light about us. But through the thick veil of the darkness of the world this is not seen or known of men, but only through the spirit may it be made clear unto us; and the spirit soars aloft rejoicing, and is girt about with delight because of it.*

And now the image of Sleep filled the orbit of my sight, and through the veil of his form I saw him who bore the mystic saffron raiment wherewith he had covered his hands. My spirit well-nigh fainting, I turned unto my Soul, and knew by the increasing glow upon him that strength was given me yet again to lift my eyes. Well was it for me that what came was revealed to me through the veil of Sleep, else I could not have borne to look upon it.

From out the uplifted hands of him who stood within the Holy Place there sprang forth a radiance of a degree so dazzling that what else of glory there was within the temple was utterly obscured; as one seeing a thin black vapour resting before the face of the mid-day sun, so I saw upon the radiance the brooding cherubim, their wings meeting, their faces hidden; I saw within the glory, one who seemed of pure snow and of pure fire, the Very Love, the Divine Type of Absolute Beauty, primaeval and eternal, compact of the white flame of youth, burning in ineffable perfection.

For a moment's space I shielded my eyes from the blinding glow, then once more raised them upon the Beatific Vision. It seemed to me as though my spirit were drawn forth from its abiding place, and dissolved in unspeakable ardours; anon fiercely whirled round in a sphere of fire, and swiftly borne along a sea of throbbing light into the Very Heart. Ah, how may words shew forth what it was then vouchsafed to me to know? As when the thin, warm tears upon the cheek of the sleeping bride are kissed away by him who knows that she is wholly his, and one with him; as softly as his trembling lips are set upon the face transfigured on his soul, even so fell upon my heart, made one with the Heart of Love, its inmost, secret flame: my spirit was wholly swallowed up, and I knew no more.

❋

Then all this wondrous vision was fulfilled, and looking upon the sky, I saw that the stars had set and the dawn had spread his wings over the world; and again the words of the sage King, *Until the day break and the shadows flee away*, came into my mind.

CLEOPATRA'S NEEDLE;
OR,
THE LABOURS OF CUPID

A Farce,
IN ONE ACT

CHARACTERS

SIR CHARLES LARKIE: A lively Young Man about Town.

CINCINNATUS BUNKUM: A great American Inventor

ABRAHAM ISAACS: A Jew Bailif

JANE BRITIAN: A bright Young Woman, come to grief from Speculation.

LADY THREADNEEDLE: A wealthy Lady, but given to Money-grubbing.

MRS. THROGMORTON: An elderly Aunt of Jane Britian's, given to the same vices as Lady Threadneedle.

CHARLOTTE: Servant to Jane Britian, sharp-tongued, and useful in the matter of Duns and Bailifs.

LODGERS, TRADESMEN, AND PORTERS.

SCENE. *A large room in a house in the neighbourhood of the Surrey Obelisk (Obelisk seen from window.) Door B. and L.; table centre; sofa, chairs, &c., neatly arranged about the room; large window, centre.*

Enter JANE, *reading a letter*, R.

JANE. "It is not because my property is in danger that I give you a week's notice. It is because I feel that the Johnsonian Establishment for Young Ladies can no longer be carried on with dignity, sobriety, and all the high culture for which this age is so conspicuous in a first floor front under which smoulders like a female volcano, a speculator who loses" (*throws herself into chair and laughs immoderately*). That's from my first floor lodger, Miss Samuelina Johnson. And now let me see what says my third floor back, Mr. Zerubbabel Smith, the Quaker, and secretary to the Self-Abnegation Building Society. (*Reads*) "It is not that my property is in danger that I give thee a week's notice; it is because thee hast been speculating and lost. Speculation is the great vice of this corrupt age-in man it is heinous, in women schoking, in landlady prodigious" (*laughs*). These good people are kind to thus turn misfortunate into a joke-ha! ha! ha!

Enter CHARLOTTE, R.

CHARLOTTE. Well, mum, for a ruined woman, your sperrits is right-on-dreadful. There's an old Jew bailif in the passage, inquiring if his son Ichabod's got here yet. He says he's sent in by your mortgagee, Lady Threadneedle. And the printer's boy from the Blackfriars Gazette has just left this (*hands* JANE *poster*).

JANE (*unfolding* poster).

No. 1,006, BLACKFRIARS STREET,
BLACKFIARS.

MR. JOHN MAMMOM
Is instructed to SELL the above LEASHOLD
HOUSE
BY AUCTION
At the MART, TOKENHOUSE YARD,
On MONDAY, DECEMBER 16TH,
At Two o'clock precisely

Particulars, with Conditions of Sale may be obtained of Messrs. DIDDLUM and TUFT, Solicitors, Gray's Inn, or of the Auctioneer.

JANE. Ah, my Lady Threadneedle, like the accomplished woman of business she is, puts into force her two remedies at once (*holds up poster*). The house my poor mother so lately left me (*voice trembles*). Let us see how we look on the hoardings of Blackfriars (*mounts chair and pins poster on wall*).

CHARLOTTE. I don't believe anything ever *would* cow you (*looking off*). Here comes the rascally American inventor, on the second floor back, who brought all this ruin about.

Enter CINCINNATUS BUNKUM, *dressed in American costume, with cigarette in his mouth, and swishing a cane,* L.

BUMKUM. Wall, young woman (*walks up to poster and looks at it*). This heear looks like a genu-ine bust-up. I guess, I must just take care of my patents, and skee-daddle afore the crows *settle*. So, if you'll make out my account slick, I'll go and fetch my cheque-book and pay up. (*Turning back*) Afore I go, however, I want to ask you one question; Who's the man in the second floor front-door opposite mine—keyhole opposite mine? (JANE *turns away in contempt.*)

CHARLOTTE. Why, that's Mr. Honour Bright, if
you *must* know, a real gentleman as 'ud scorn takin'
advantage of a poor young woman, and cheat her
out of her money. And there's no need for you to
watch *him* about for fear he should find out your
patents. *He* don't want your patents, *I'm* sure. Here
he comes.

Enter SIR CHARLES LARKIE (*with open letter*).

BUNKUM and SIR CHARLES (*together*). Wall, tell
Mr. Honour Bright tell Mr. Cincinnatus Bunkum—
that if I catch him spying so close to my keyhole, I'll
just (*they stop, and look at each other menacingly*).
Exit BUNKUM.

SIR CHARLES (*laughing*). So that's the great inventor, is it? (*To* JANE) Good afternoon, Miss Britain.

JANE (*bowing*). Good afternoon, Mr. Honour Bright.

SIR CHARLES. Now, am I really to take this notice
to quit as final (*showing paper*).

JANE. Yes, sir.

SIR CHARLES. It is very cruel. What have I done?
(*To* CHARLOTTE) Charlotte, you can go.

JANE. It was the greatest mistake my servant letting
you the rooms at all. *I* should have seen at once
that they were not for such as you.

SIR CHARLES. Not for such as I. Don't add insult to injury. I'm not good enough, I suppose, for the second. floor? Have you got a sixth? Charlotte, my bed wants making.

CHARLOTTE. (*Aside*) Confound the man.

Exit L.

JANE. In one sense, too good; in another sense, not good enough. To be quite plain with you, I don't think your name is Honour Bright at all.

SIR CHARLES. Oh! honour bright!

JANE. I perceived, as soon as I saw you, that you were the same gentleman who at the Monday Popular Concerts so far forgot yourself as to——

SIR CHARLES. Fall in love with your look of piquancy and dauntless pluck, and seek you out. Well, it is too true. I am the scoundrel in question. But is that a reason for turning me out like a dog into the streets—homeless—(for *you* are my home), and a beggar (for without *you* my soul starves)?

JANE. Reason enough. But, if another were wanted, the bailiffs are in, and look here (*pointing to sale bill*).

SIR CHARLES. I say! I'm very grieved for this, though—I really am. What does it all mean?

What's the amount? I'll pay the fellows out, or else I'll go and kick 'em out (*puts his arm round her waist*).

JANE (*releasing herself*). No, sir. It's very good of you. I feel that you *are* good, in spite of looking the most impudent man in London; but, of course, it is impossible that you should pay out my bailiffs.

SIR CHARLES. Hang Mrs. Grundy. She is ubiquitous. I *did* think that in Blackfriars—but never mind: even *she* would not object to my kicking them out. Where are they? (*Going.* JANE *pulls him back laughing.*) By the bye, what did your servant mean about the rascally American? Has he been cheating you? If he has, a drop from the second floor window might improve his morals, and I shall be—

JANE(*with great heat*). He persuaded me to invest all my mother's legacy in his patents, and what was worse, to mortgage the lease of this house to supply money for his schemes.

SIR CHARLES (*again putting his arm around her waist, and trying to kiss her*) I'll try the window with him, and kick the bailiffs out—kick everybody out. There's no need for more than us two here. We want no servants. *I* can light the fires, and you cook, or somebody here does—a deviled kidney or more (*screwing up his face*)—devilishly well!

JANE (*repulsing him*). Will you leave me, sir? (*looking at him*). *Do* leave me, now, there's a good fellow. I'm certain you are a good fellow (he again tries to kiss her). Oh! if you could only make that rascally American disgorge my money, you might——

SIR CHARLES. What?

JANE. I do so want to conquer him. And I do so want to see these bailiffs turned out with *his* money; and, if my house *must* be sold, I want to sell it myself. Then I shouldn't care: the world's wide, and I am young. I will go to Australia, where women are not quite such a drug.

SIR CHARLES (*aside*). What a look of pluck there is in the girl's eyes! (*To* JANE) Agreed. The Yankee's neck shall be spared in order that he may disgorge: the bailiffs shall skeedaddle, and you shall be your own auctioneer—I swear it. And *you* will keep your part of the compact?

JANE (*laughing*). I will. I know I am perfectly safe.

SIR CHARLES. Don't be too confident.

JANE. I fancy you outwitting the "smartest man in America," as he is called, I believe. And he is rich, they say, as well as smart.

SIR CHARLES. Don't defy Cupid, he is stronger than Hercules when he takes his labours in earnest. He has entered this frame. He inspires me. The Labours of Cupid are begun.

Re-enter CHARLOTTE, *with a boy carrying cold roast fowl, a basket of champagne, a box of cigars, and some wine-glasses,* R.

CHARLOTTE. These are for you, sir. I will take them upstairs at once.

SIR CHARLES. Hulloa! I recollect I did order a snack at the Blue Lion. (*To* boy) You can call again for the champagne basket.

Exit BOY.

CHARLOTTE. The third basket of Blue Lion gooseberry-wine this week (*sets basket down*).

SIR CHARLES. The fact is there's something wrong about Blackfriars air. Its action upon the throat is to produce a state of chronic thirst. Even at this moment I feel I must drink champagne or perish. As my moments are numbered here, would you allow me to draw just one valedictory cork?

JANE. What are those papers you have, Charlotte?

CHARLOTTE. A boy from the *Blackfriars Gazette* Office brought this newspaper and note, and he's to wait for an answer (JANE *reads letter and then turns to newspaper and reads paragraph, while* SIR CHARLES *uncorks a bottle of champagne*).

SIR CHARLES. Charlotte, glasses! (CHARLOTTE *hands three glasses*). Three! Oh, yes, there are three of us (*fills three glasses, hands one to* JANE *as she reads, the other to* CHARLOTTE). Have you been long a drinker of champagne, Charlotte?

CHARLOTTE (*empting her glass with a grimace*). Long enough to know it from this.

SIR CHARLES (*aside*). Well, May Fair is impudent; but it has no idea what it could learn from Blackfriars.

JANE. What a shame! The lady alluded to there (*handing* SIR CHARLES *paper*) is my aunt. She's ignorant, poor old thing! but she shan't be made a public butt.

SIR CHARLES. She shan't (*reading aloud*):—

"CLEOPATRA'S NEEDLE: THE BATTLE OF THE SITES.—It is a wonderful fact that an old and wealthy lady, residing not a thousand miles from the Obelisk, has got the maggot into her head that the authorities will decide to erect Cleopatra's Needle in sight of the Surrey Obelisk, because according to Dr. Erasmus Wilson's pamphlet, the

Needle 'stood with a companion' near a temple in the Egyptian city of On."

SIR CHARLES. I confess I don't see the joke. It's certainly the least ridiculous site proposed yet.

JANE. The editor sends me this letter. You may as well see that too (*hands* SIR CHARLES *letter*).

SIR CHARLES (*reading letter aloud*):—

"Blackfriars Gazette Office, Dec., 1877.
DEAR MADAM, The paragraph I have marked has been sent to us. At the last moment, before going to press, it has occurred to me that you, as an esteemed friend and subscriber, ought to see the proof of the paper. I am just going out, but should you find the personal allusion to your aunt offensive to *yourself*, you can strike it out, and my compositor will fill in the space with something else. The bearer will wait———. Yours truly JAMES BABBAGE, *Editor*.

CHARLOTTE (*To* SIR CHARLES). They call her "Money-grubbing Sal."

JANE. Shall I be offended? he asks. Of course I shall (*pulls out pencil, strikes out words in pencil*). There! I have struck out all allusion to my aunt, and not taken out much either (*hands paper to* CHARLOTTE, *but* SIR CHARLES *takes it, and reads, while* CHARLOTTE *and* JANE *converse at back*).

SIR CHARLES (*aside*). Yes, you have struck out all allusion to your aunt! and, should the printer let it appear as it stands, there will be all the tradesmen of Blackfriars speculating in sites for Cleopatra's Needle near the Obelisk! (*Reads*) "It is a wonderful fact that the authorities will decide to erect Cleopatra's Needle in sight of the Surrey Obelisk, because according to Dr. Erasmus Wilson's pamphlet, the Needle 'stood with a companion' near a temple in the Egyptian city of On". Well, I won't tell her. This, perhaps be turned to account in the Labours of Cupid, though I don't at present see how.

CHARLOTTE (*to* JANE). Well, all I can say is, I wish you had let the newspapers have their laugh at her, an old——

JANE. Silence, Charlotte! You seem to forget she is my aunt.

SIR CHARLES. And, if your mistress's, mine.

CHARLOTTE. And you seem to forget that she cheated you out of the legacy you ought to have had under your grand-father's will.

SIR CHARLES. Do tell me about this aunt. I am so interested always in aunts. I've one myself, spinsterial, rich, eternal. But, Charlotte, hadn't you better take that newspaper to the printer's devil?

CHARLOTTE (*aside*). Oh, yes, of course! Wants to be alone again with her. But you can't help liking him: he's got such an impudent look.

Exit L.

SIR CHARLES (drawing up to JANE). What is the meaning of this new maggot of the moneygrub genus which has attacked your—aunt?

JANE (*slyly*). As you are so very much interested, I will tell you; and then you must and shall act at once on my notice to quit.

SIR CHARLES (*handing a glass of wine to* JANE). Yes; (*aside*) it's the look of fun dancing up in her eyes that crazes me.

JANE (*laughing*). Well, ever since the railway, some years ago, paid her such an enormous amount of compensation-money for the site of her house at Camberwell, her head has been quite turned about buying up sites and obtaining compensation-money; and since she went to see the Lord Mayor's Show the other week, a money-grub, as you call it, has attacked her of a very peculiar kind in connexion with Cleopatra's Needle and the Battle of the Sites. She is very illiterate, but in Dr. Erasmus Wilson's little pamphlet about Cleopatra's Needle she is quite learned.

SIR CHARLES. How very interesting. I knew I should be rewarded if I stopped. Is she much like you?

JANE (*laughing*). Well, I hope not! But she's my only relative, and as a forlorn hope I sent for her a little while since. I am expecting her now (*bell rings outside*). Here she is, I dare say. So good-bye.

SIR CHARLES. Oh, if she's actually at the door, I can't be so rude as to bolt out, the moment——

Re-enter CHARLOTTE, *followed by two men carrying a package about five feet six inches high, wrapped in a packing-cloth,* L.

CHARLOTTE. These men from the Parcels Delivery Company have brought this, and insist upon leaving it (*the men place it in the middle of room*).

JANE (*going up to it, and reading address*). There's no name on the card; only the number of the house.

PORTER. Number of the house means *landlady* of the house. Are *you* the landlady, mum, because if you are, we must leave it with you, unless you say you won't take it.

SIR CHARLES. Yes; we're the landlady (*to* JANE). Don't send it away.

JANE (*to* PORTER). You can leave it. (PORTER *presents parcel-book for signature.* JANE *signs.*) *Exeunt Porters* L.

JANE and CHARLOTTE (*together*). Whatever can it be? (*They and* SIR CHARLES *walk round it.*)

JANE. I certainly thought it moved. It looks to me a man.

SIR CHARLES. A man? (*feels it*) The feminine wish is father to the thought—feels more like a woman (*pulls out penknife, and thrusts it into parcel*). Breast as hard as a money-lender's (*shakes it*). It isn't a box of money. I give it up.

JANE (*to* SIR CHARLES). I wonder if it's anything of yours; not another man introduced I hope in a "long pack."

SIR CHARLES. Another man! The very last thing I should introduce here! That it's not another *woman* I perceive by the instinctive interest you show in it. Inference, it is of the neuter gender. Fetch a knife, Charlotte (CHARLOTTE *runs* R. *out, and returns with carving-knife and ordinary dinner-knife, runs to package with it, and gives* JANE *a large table-knife.*

They begin to rip open the cloth. An envelope falls out, which SIR CHARLES *picks up unperceived by them, and takes to front of stage.*)

JANE and CHARLOTTE (*together, with excitement*). It is alive! It is a man! Mind how you cut. Here's his whiskers! Here's his mouth! Ha! It's one of the Lord Mayor's Sphinxes! (*They pull off cloth, and disclose a model of Cleopatra's Needle, ornamented with hieroglyphic figures painted on false sides or shutters, working with hinges. Near the top there is a face in high relief, removable for business, of an Egyptian Sphinx. The Obelisk has on one side a practicable door.*)

SIR CHARLES. Great fall in the price of gingerbread! Lord Mayor selling off!

JANE *and* CHARLOTTE (*together*). Cleopatra's Needle, with one of the Lord Mayor's Sphinx' heads! What can it mean? What's in it?

SIR CHARLES (*aside, reading paper*). Oh! oh! Here's a god-send. I'll pass this model off as mine, and tell her leave without taking my property with me. It'll give me another day here. It's evidently something for the scoundrel Yankee upstairs (*reads while* JANE *and* CHARLOTTE *are busy inspecting Needle*):—

"To Cincinnatus Bunkum, Esq.'
DEAR SIR,—Owing to the unexpected return of our modeller from Paris, we have the great pleasure to send you a week earlier than we had promised, the model of your new invention, the Patent Walking Advertisement Obelisk, and return your written instructions. We thought it well to address it your house merely—partly because the name of so famous an inventor might have excited the curiosity of our men, but chiefly because you alluded to being under the surveillance of a spy in the second floor of the house you live in.

"Yours obediently,
    "SMUDGE and TINKLER."

(*Looks at Needle, then takes from envelope instructions.*)
Ho, ho! Now I will read the patentee's instructions, to see if Messrs. Smudge and Tinkler have done justice to Mr. Bunkum's inventive genius (*reads*):
"Each side of the Obelisk is to be furnished with a false side or shutter, ornamented according to pattern, upon hinges—so that when the sandwich man inside pulls a string they fly open, and disclose the true sides displaying advertisements. The Sphinx's face to be moveable from within, so that the sandwich man can replace it by his own face at will."
So this is the last new thing in advertisement sandwiches! Well; the idea's so very original, that is to say, so very bunkum that the British investors *must*

come down on it as thick as flies. So, I'm a spy, am I? I'd no idea I was anything half so clever. But to the smart man all the world is smart. He doesn't expect it home for a week! Meantime, it shall be mine. (*Walks up to Needle.*) Where's the fastening? Oh! here it is. (*Touches catch, when door flies open. He enters, pulls the door to, while* JANE *and* CHARLOTTE, *in amazement, look on. He then removes from, within the Sphinx' face, and shows his own surrounded by the Sphinx's headpiece.* JANE *and* CHARLOTTE *shriek with astonishment.*)

JANE. Then that extraordinary thing is yours?

SIR CHARLES. Could you doubt it?

JANE (*laughing*). No, no. Such a whimsical thing could only have been invented by you. I never saw anything so characteristic. It really *is* yours?

SIR CHARLES. If the product of a man's own inventive brain may be called his—then the Patent Walking Advertisement Obelisk may be called mine; otherwise, there are infernal pirating Yankee inventors roaming the earth who would no more mind peeping through my keyhole, pirating my idea, and——

JANE. Then you are not a gentleman after all, but only an inventor like the American

SIR CHARLES. I am proud to find Blackfriars so apt at distinctions. I am only an inventor. Now, may I stay?

JANE (*bell rings*). That must be my aunt. Come with me, Charlotte. (*To* SIR CHARLES.) If you won't leave the house, at least go to your own apartments.
Exeunt JANE *and* CHARLOTTE L.

SIR CHARLES (*coming from Needle*). That girl's turning my head fast. She's as fearless as an English lady, and as brilliant as a French——(*listens*). Hulloa! Somebody's coming along the passage. The Yankee, most likely. I must hide this, somehow (*runs to packing-cloth*). No time! I'll get behind the Obelisk, and attack him in ambush (*slips behind Needle*).

Enter ICHABOD, *with inventory—book open, and pencil in hand,* L.

ICHABOD. I yonder vere my father is. He told me to come first and begin the inventory. I vent to the second floor, and an American came to the door with a bowie-knife, and pitched me downstairs for being near his keyhole. I hope it ishn't madhouse they've sent us to, but it looks like it (*sees Needle*). Vy, vot ish dish? Dish looksh very mad (*goes up to it, raps it, opens door*). Yesh, dish does look *very* mad. I yonder vot's inside (*gets into Needle, and inspects it*).

SIR CHARLES (*coming forward, and shutting door of Needle, and catching it*). Ha! Ha! We've killed the keeper, and the cook boils in his own pot.

ICHABOD. Murder! murder!

SIR CHARLES (*looking out of door, and listening*). There's some one else coming along the passage. This, of course, is the Yankee, and he'll see his invention, after all, before I can turn it to account (runs to packing-cloth, mounts chair, and throws it over top of model, which now looks something like a coffin).

ICHABOD (*kicking within*). Murder! murder!

SIR CHARLES (*in his natural voice*). Hold your row, you fool! The mad people are all upon us (*aside*). Now, I'm ready to receive my Yankee. Why, this is the parent bailiff!

Enter ABRAHAM ISAACS, *an old man, bowing to* SIR CHARLES, L.

ISAACS. Vot vash dat noish? I thought I heard somebody cry murder. I yonder were is my son Ichabod, vot I sent on here fust with the execution to take the inventory. I cannot find Ichabod.

SIR CHARLES. Oh, you are the bailiff? (ISAACS *grins and bows*.) Walk in, bailiff (ISAACS *advances*).

ISAACS (*pointing to package*). Vot is dat? It looks very like the best bed packed up to ne taken off. We can't allow dat, unless you (*grins*).

SIR CHARLES (*confidentially*). Best bed stuffed with spoons. Shut the door, bailiff (ISAACS *shuts door*); bolt it, bailiff (*he bolts it*). Come along, bailiff (ISAACS *advances*). (*In a solemn, meaning tone.*) Did anybody see you enter the house?

ISAACS. No, ve always slips in vidout being seen.

SIR CHARLES. All right, bailiff. It's *my* business to take that that nobody sees you go *out*, bailiff (*stoops and picks up carving knife*).

ICHABOD (*kicks the box*). Oh! I shall be smothered (ISAACS *starts back*).

JEW. Vot ish dat noise? And vy do you pick up that knife?

SIR CHARLES (*stoops, picks up poker and sharpens knife on it.* ISAACS, *alarmed, retreats:* SIR CHARLES *moves between him and the door*). Come here on the oil-cloth (*beckons him*). I hope you're not as full as *he* was, bailiff (*pointing to package*).

ISAACS. Full of vot?

SIR CHARLES. Blood, bailiff.

ISAACS (*aghast, pointing to package*). Den vot is dat?

SIR CHARLES. Inside that coffin, bailiff it *was* a
bailiff.

ICHABOD (*kicking in Needle*). Murder, murder!
Father, help!

SIR CHARLES. Don't be frightened. It seems he
wasn't quite dead when we put him in.

ISAACS (*shrieking*). Who? Ichabod?

SIR CHARLES. Oh! was that his name Well, Ichabod
(*brandishing knife to Needle*), *you* spoilt our best
carpet. I'll take care this one don't: come to the
oil-cloth (*collars him*).

ICHABOD. They've killed the keeper! and the cook's
being boiled in his own pot!

ISAACS (*struggling violently*). Oh, a mad house!
Murder, murder! Let me go! I'm very full of
blood—very full of blood indeed, for an old
man—fuller of blood than Ichabod! I shall spile de
carpet. I shall soak right through de floor, I shall.
Murder, murder! Let me go! (*extricates himself*).

JANE *is heard at door*, L.

SIR CHARLES. Well, if you're so full of blood as *that*, you'll be a nuisance here. I can hear the lady of the house coming this way. I don't want the bother of sticking you; I've stuck so many. Perhaps she might spare your life if you asked her in a proper way.

ISAACS. Vot shall I do, sir? Vot shall I do?

SIR CHARLES. Oh, I leave that to you. *I* know what *I* should do.

JEW. Vot should *you* do, sir?

SIR CHARLES. Well, I should fall on my knees when she comes in. I should empty my pockets, lay my money on the floor before her and say, "This will help to pay out the bailiff." Then, in my very prettiest manner, I should ask her to let me go, and promise to never come back.

Re-enter JANE, L.

ISAACS (*approaching her, and falling on his knees*). Oh, good lady, let me go, let me go! I vill never come back here any more—never any more! Never, never! Let me go, let me go!

JANE (*in bewilderment*). Certainly, you may go if you like, and I am not particularly anxious for your return.

128

ISAACS (*emptying his pockets, and laying money on floor*). This vill help to pay out the bailiffs (*rising and rushing to door*). Bless you, lady! bless you, lady!

Exit L.

JANE (*looking at money, picking it up, and then at* SIR CHARLES). Why, what can this mean?

SIR CHARLES. The labours of Cupid. The love-god talked to the old man so eloquently about the iniquity of his calling, that—well you see the result of Cupid's eloquence.

JANE (*looking at* SIR CHARLES *in amazement*). Wonderful man!

SIR CHARLES (*advancing towards her*). And Cupid will win! (*kisses her*).

JANE (*shrinking back*). But this money! This is, of course, some mistake. I must follow this convert of Cupid's, and at least make him take back his money.

Exit R.

SIR CHARLES (*goes to door, L., and unbolts it. Then walks up to Needle, and opens door*). Well, I'm glad one of you has escaped. I thought they would have killed the old man. What made the sheriff send you here?

ICHABOD. This is a private madhouse, and you are
the keeper?

SIR CHARLES. With the perspicacity of your race,
you have struck the nail at once.

ICHABOD. And you locked me in there to save my
life?

SIR CHARLES. Again does the Hebraic acuteness
pierce to the truth like lightning. But spare your
expressions of gratitude. You are quite welcome.
What a strong prejudice mad people have against
Jew bailiffs! It's very strange.

ICHABOD. Then they've broken loose?

SIR CHARLES. Yes; I think it was the sight of your father's nose that irritated them. The mad American
cried out, "Sickle, sickle" and sprang upon him.
That's the man with the craze about keyholes and
inventions, who, I believe, threatened you on the
second floor with a bowie-knife for being near
his key-hole. The mad old English woman, with
the craze about Cleopatra's Needle and the Surrey
Obelisk, followed suit; and, last of all, the young
woman with the money-craze rushed in. I just got
here at the nick of time.

ICHABOD. For God's sake let me get out of this.

SIR CHARLES. I can't. They are all over the house (*listens*). I fancy I can hear the money-maniac coming this way now, poor thing! She mostly uses a carving-knife like that (*pointing to knife on floor*).

ICHABOD. Vot am I to do?

SIR CHARLES. Oh, they're all easily managed, if you know them. Empty pockets before this one, and she's as gentle as a lamb. How much money have you got about you?

ICHABOD (*digging his hands in his pockets*). Fifty-five pounds. I have just taken it from an execution paid out.

SIR CHARLES. Well, other people's money is just as good as your own for all practical purposes. When she comes in, kneel before her; lay the money at her feet and say, "This will help to pay out the bailiffs." She is a *lady*, and will take it as a touchingly graceful act as coming *from* a bailiff.

Enter JANE *and* CHARLOTTE.

JANE. I can do nothing with this extraordinary old man. (*Bell rings in passage.*)

CHARLOTTE (*running off*). This must be your aunt, at last.

JANE. He positively refuses to take the money, and has gone away without it. Now, what *does* it mean?

ICHABOD (*advancing to* JANE, *kneeling, emptying his pockets, and laying money at her feet*). This vill help to pay out the bailiffs.

JANE. Well, this is most bewildering (*aside*). This brilliant madcap is sending the world mad. I wonder who he is.

Enter CHARLOTTE, L.

CHARLOTTE. Your aunt is here—umbrella and all. *She's* no good. She looks as black as Newgate.

Exeunt JANE *and* CHARLOTTE, L.

ICHABOD (*to* SIR CHARLES). I've got out of *that* one. She seems to know she's mad, poor thing! Vill the others come?

SIR CHARLES. Sure to.

ICHABOD. What am I to do?

SIR CHARLES. All you've got to do is to go back into that Needle, and shut yourself in (*leads him to Needle, puts him inside, and removes Sphinx's face*). Here! you see this string. If the American comes, all you have to do is to walk about, pull that string, and, whenever he speaks, say "Keyhole!" He considers "Keyhole" to mean "God bless you." If it's the old woman with the Obelisk craze, she's very touchy; your best way, perhaps, would be to stand still, and humour her by expressing your agreement with everything she says. If she asks a question, for instance, answer it by repeating exactly her own words. I've often found this to be the only way of humouring her. *Her* weapon is mostly—an umbrella, of the gingham species I think; but she *can* use her teeth.

ICHABOD. Oh, Lord! Oh, Lord! If I only get out of this place——

SIR CHARLES. You will never return to it, you were about to say. I cannot say that your resolution is impolitic (*going*).

ICHABOD. Oh, don't go, sir.

SIR CHARLES. I shall be back in a minute (*aside*). I must just go and see that there is no exposé with the old Jew. I hope he is clear off.

Exit L.

ICHABOD (*listening to noise in passage*). Lord! Lord! there's somebody coming (Mrs. THROGMOR-TON *is heard storming loudly in the passage and approaching. She enters* R., *she is asthmatic, and carries a large umbrella*). It's the old woman with the gingham. I've got to agree with all she says.

MRS. THROGMORTON (*storming in a very loud and angry voice*). Just what I thought and said. Whenever nieces want to see aunts "*very* particular," it's allus to drag money out on 'em—*allus!* Not a word do I hear from you till your house is goin' to be sold, and you're broke, then it's "Aunty, dear, come forrud!" "Aunty, dear," *allus* means comin' forrud, and allus means bein' money-dragged. But I ain't a-goire to come forrud, and I ain't a-goin' to be money-dragged (*sees poster*). Oh! this is the bill, then, as she said wur up on the wall, is it? (*goes up to poster*). She couldn't tell me neither the date nor the place of sale. Rare bisness head! Jest like her mother as is dead and gone; only *she* didn't set up to be the fine lady. I *will* say that for her. Eddication's a cuss (*reads poster*). Ah now! if *this* was a-goin' to be the site of Cleopatra's Needle—and it may be, for the paper I bought coming along (*pulling out "Blackfriars Gazette"*) says they have decided to put it near the Surrey Obelisk, after all their laughing at me (*turns round and sees Needle*). Why, bless me, ain't that the moral of Cleopatra's Needle as Goveement's a puttin' up all ovor Londen?

ICHABOD (*from Needle*). It's the moral of Cleopatra's Needle as Government's a puttin' up all over London.

MRS. THROGMORTON (*aside*). Bless me, what voice is that? I hope my sister don't haunt this house (*moves round as to see* ICHABOD' S *face*). It's alive! Thieves! Thieves!

ICHABOD. It's alive! Thieves! Thieves!

MRS. THROGMORTON (*in amazement*). You call *me* thieves? Do you? What do you mean by calling me thieves? Of course, I'm alive.

ICHABOD. You call *me* thieves? do you? Vot do you mean by calling me thieves? Of course, I'm alive.

MRS. THROGMORTON (*aside*). I wonder what this means. Lord! if it should mean that the Goveement's trying this very house of Jane's for the site of Cleopatra's Needle. (*To* ICHABOD) Are you the Gover'ment, sir.

ICHABOD. I am the Goveement, mum.

MRS. THROGMORTON (*aside*), Perhaps it's the Prime Minister himself come to look at the Surrey Obelisk out of the winder, to see if the two will match. Are you the Prime Minister, sir?

ICHABOD. I am the Prime Minister, mum.

MRS. THROGMORTON. And are you the Sphinx, too, sir?

ICHABOD. And I am the Sphinx, too, mum.

MRS. THROGMORTON. Is that the Gover'ment's Needle, sir?

ICHABOD. This is the Gover'ment's Needle, mum.

MRS. THROGMORTON (*aside*). How straightforward he answers questions, to be sure! And he a Prime Minister and a Sphinx! Is this house selected as the site of Cleopatra's Needle, sir?

ICHABOD. This house is selected as the site of Cleopatra's needle, mum.

MRS. THROGMORTON (*with great excitement*). To be a Companion for the Surrey Obelisk, sir?

ICHABOD. To be a companion for the Surrey Obelisk, mum.

MRS. THROGMORTON (*aside*). I know'd it! I know'd it! But to think that the site I've been lookin' arter should turn out to be Jane's house, arter all. (*Aside, with trembling eagerness*) I must buy it of Jane, afore she knows what's the vally on it; (*in a despairing tone*) but, then, it's up for sale, and everybody will be buyin' it, and gettin' thousands for compensation. Oh! what *shall* I do? what *shall* I do? what *shall* I do? (*To* ICHABOD) Oh, sir! I'm Jane's aunt—her only pertecter, now her poor mother's dead and gone. This property's up for sale.

There's the bill (*pointing to poster*). It'll be bought right over the family's heads, and that'll break the family's hearts. What shall I do? I can pay off the mortgage money, can't I?

ICHABOD. You can pay off the mortgage money, can't you?

MRS. THHOGMORTON. Of course I can, sir.

ICHABOD. Of course you can, mum.

MRS. THROGMORTON. I can give Lady Threadneedle notice at once to pay her off before the sale. I'm Jane's aunt, sir. Of course I am.

ICHABOD. You can give Lady Threadneedle notice at once to pay her off before the sale. You're Jane's aunt, mum. Of course you are.

MRS. THROGMORTON. How straightforrud his answers are, to be sure! And he a Prime Minister and a Sphinx! (*Runs to table and turns over pens and paper*) Oh, but I'm such a dreadful bad writer, sir!

ICHABOD. Oh, but you're such a dreadful bad writer, mum! (SIR CHARLES'S *footsteps are heard approaching in passage*).

MRS. THROGMORTON. Perhaps here's somebody coming as can write it for me.

ICHABOD. Perhaps here's somebody coming as can write it for you.

Re-enter SIR CHARLES, L.

MRS. THROGMORTON I dare say he belongs to the Gover'ment's, too, sir.

ICHABOD. I dare say, he belongs to the Gover'ment's, too, mum.

MRS. THROGMORTON (*approaching* SIR CHARLES). Oh, sir, this property as is going to be taken by the Gover'ment's for the site of Cleopatra's Needle is going to be sold by a wicked old lady named Lady Threadneedle for her mortgage money, and I'm Jane's aunt, sir.

SIR CHARLES. The deuce you are! (*Aside*) Fancy, my charmer with an aunt like this. Oh, that Beauty had no family connexions!

MRS. THROGMORTON. And I want to pay off her mortgage money, and this gentleman says he's the Prime Minister, and a Sphinx, too; and he says of course I can pay it off if I like bein' her aunt, and he says you belong to the Gover'ment, and he's quite sure you will be so kind as to write out the notices for me, because, he says, I'm such a bad writer.

SIR CHARLES (*looking in amazement at* ICHABOD). Well! at the long bow I thought Cupid had been just displaying a pretty firm hand; but for real masterly archery, give me a Prime Minister, as is a Sphinx, too.

MRS. THROGMORTON. Oh, sir, please write it out at once. Here's the *Blackfriars Gazette* got wind of it, and they'll be comin' about us like a shoal o' herrings to buy it over our heads (*shows him paragraph in "Blackfriars Gazette"*).

SIR CHARLES (*taking newspaper and reading paragraph, aside*). Why, it really is so. The stupid compositor has actually printed the paragraph exactly as Jane altered it; but, still, it doesn't indicate the exact spot selected for the site. Perhaps (*meaningly*) I had better indicate it for them in this elegant aunt's notice of postponement of sale. (*To* MRS. THROGMORTON) Then you are ready to pay her off?

MRS. THROGMORTON. Yes, yes.

SIR CHARLES. Pardon me, madam; the Government, to be a Government at all, must be practical. Did the Prime Minister (*pointing to* ICHABOD) put the financial question: How are you off for tin?

ICHABOD. How are you off for tin, mum?

MRS. THROGMORTON. Do you mean money? I've just been taking my Michaelmas rents, and I've got a goodish bit just now.

SIR CHARLES. A goodish bit meaning?—

MRS. THROGMORTON. Three hundred and fifty-six pound, six shillings.

SIR CHARLES. Is it in the bank?

MRS. THROGMORTON. Some's in the bank, and some's in a worsted stockin'.

SIR CHARLES. Bring the stocking here, and while the Prime Minister and I count the contents, you must send a notice immediately to Lady Threadneedle (for she, I believe, is the mortgagee) that you, as Miss Britain's aunt, are ready to pay her off. Shall I write the notice for you?

MRS. THROGMORTON. Oh, if you would be so kind, sir. (*Aside*) I shall make thousands by this if Jane don't find it out too soon.

SIR CHARLES (*sits down and writes, reading out to himself*). "My Lady, I beg to give you notice that I shall, within one week of this date, pay off, on behalf of my niece, Miss Jane Britain, the full amount of principal, interest, and costs, due to you in respect of your mortgage upon No. 1,006,

Blackfriars Street, Blackfriars. No doubt you have heard that the house has been selected as the site of Cleopatra's Needle." (*Aside*) Lady Threadneedle is very energetic. I am mistaken in her business capacity and rapacity if she does not fly hither to buy the site. And this notice I have been preparing for the aunt to sign (reads) "SALE POSTPONED ON ACCOUNT OF THE SITE HAVING BEEN SELECTED FOR CLEOPATRA'S NEEDLE," will, if posted over the sale bill, tend also to enliven the market, and prevent so valuable a property from being thrown away. Madam, if you'll sit down and sign these (*rises and directs her to take his place*).

MRS. THROGMORTON (*sitting down*). Don't look at me, please. I ain't much of a writer at the best o' times; and now I'm a little excited, the pen won't stir if you look at it.

SIR CHARLES. Then, I'll look another way.

ICHABOD. How dreadful mad *she* seems, sir.

SIR CHARLES. Dreadful.

ICHABOD. I suppose she ain't really goin' out of the house, sir.

SIR CHARLES. Of course not.

ICHABOD. You managed her wonderful well, sir,

SIR CHARLES. Experience, nothing more. (MRS.
THROGMORTON *rises.*) Have you quite done?

MRS. THROGMORTON (*with a sigh of relief*).
Quite, sir.

SIR CHARLES. Sure?

MRS. THROGMORTON. Yes, sir. It's all done.

SIR CHARLES. That's right (*folding up and directing
letters*). Now, this letter to Lady Threadneedle you
must give to a hansom cabman outside. Pay him
his full fare—half-a-crown; tell him to drive as
hard as he can to this address.

MRS. THROGMORTON. Yes, sir. I'll keep that in
this hand.

SIR CHARLES. Then take this letter to the nearest
printers.

MRS. THROGMORTON. That's the *Gazette* office.

SIR CHARLES. Tell him to print this at once, and
distribute the bills. Then go home, get the stocking, put it in your pocket, and bring it to me.

MRS. THROGMORTON. Yes, sir; I'll put *them* in
this hand (*is going*).

SIR CHARLES. Stop a moment. Besides the stocking money, have you any other loose cash in the house?

MRS. THROGMORTON. I've got ten pounds, but it ain't loose; it's in the bureau secret drawer.

SIR CHARLES. Ten pounds! That's all?

MRS. THROGMORTON. Yes, sir; that's all.

SIR CHARLES. Then that must do, I suppose. *That* you will bring also and hand over to me as the Government's Needle fee.

THROGMORTON. Did you say Needle fee, sir?

SIR CHARLES. Needle fee.

MRS. THROGMORTON. Oh, Needle fee, Needle, Needle fee.

Exit L.

SIR CHARLES (*aside*). Cupid is getting on. He will make the old girl disgorge the grandfather's legacy, too.

MRS. THROGMORTON (*returning*). What did you say the Needle fee was for, sir?

SIR CHARLES. That's for advertising the postponement of the sale on the Government Needle;
like this (*opening the false sides, and showing the
advertisements*).

MRS. THROGMORTON (*going*). Oh, I see, sir;
Needle fee, Needle fee.

Exit L.

SIR CHARLES. What a splendid scoundrel Cupid is
making of me! Inspired as I am, it is a shame for
me to be an idle man about town when Scotland-
yard is crying out for talent.

ICHABOD. It's wonderful how you managed her.

SIR CHARLES. Experience, I assure you. Should they
imprison you in that Needle for only a week, you
will be quite as clever with them. (*Aside*) I must
follow the old woman, though, and see that she
doesn't jostle her niece.

Exit L.

ICHABOD. He's left me alone again. (*Listens*) And,
oh Lord, oh Lord, oh Lord, here comes the other
madman. Here's the American as is mad about
keyholes. Let me see; vot am I to do with him. Oh,
I recollect; I'm to say "Keyhole," which, he thinks,
means God bless you, and pull this string, and valk
about.

144

Enter CINCINNATUS BUNKUM, *with cheque-book in his hand,* L.

BUNKUM. Wall, young woman, if you've made out my account, I'll jis draw you a cheque. But let me see the figgers first. They say a Cockney gal, when she is smart, will jest chop down a New York gal afore she can pull out *her* chopper. (*Turns round, sees Needle; stands transfixed* by ICHABOD'S *eyes; walks up to it as if drawn by fascination; then stops, and looks round room, as though to satisfy himself where he is.*) Wall, Sphinx, I don't know who you air, but you've chopped *me* down (*looks round room again*).

ICHABOD (*from Needle*). Keyhole! (*He moves about room pulling the string, and displaying advertisements.*)

BUNKUM (*starting back*). Damnation! The second floor front!

ICHABOD. Keyhole! (*Proceeds to walk about room as before.*) Keyhole!

BUNKUM(*shaking his fist at* ICHABOD). That's the hook nose I saw against my door. A conspiracy! Come out of it! come out of it! (*Pulls out his bowie-knife.*)
"I'll drop a slice of liver or tew,
My bloomin' shrub, with yew."

ICHABOD (*walking about*). Keyhole! keyhole! keyhole!

Re-enter JANE *and* CHARLOTTE, L.

CHARLOTTE (*screaming*). I declare here's Mr. Honour Bright's new invention walking about!

JANE (*aside*). Oh, don't be frightened. He's put some man in it to try it.

BUNKUM (*sarcastically, putting up his knife*). So that's Mr. Honour Bright's invention, is it?

JANE. Of course, it is.

CHARLOTTE. Unless you manage to steal it before he can make it safe. But I dare say you will.

BUNKUM. And what name does Mr. Honour Bright give to his invention?

JANE. The Patent Walking Advertisement Obelisk.

BUNKUM. Oh! that's what he calls it, is it! And what's the principle of it?

JANE. Oh, he showed us that. (*Aside*) I see how it is, I think. Mr. Honour Bright has forestalled his patent. Won't I tease him? (*holding out her hand in an oratorical manner.* ICHABOD *keeps walking about and saying, "Keyhole!"*) We are to consider that the man inside is a sandwich man, carrying this patent Obelisk about London. The attraction of the hieroglyphics, and especially of the Sphinx's head, will be immense, Mr. Bunkum, immense. All London will be at the heels of the sandwich man. Then, at the moment when the excitement is at the very hottest, he pulls a string inside, and, presto! all the sides of the Needle fly open as they now are, and disclose advertisements paid for beforehand at enormous and unprecedented rates.

BUNKUM. Oh, that's the principle of it! And now all I want to do is to see the great inventor, and (*grating his teeth*) jest teach him carvin.'

JANE. Oh, here comes Mr. Honour Bright himself.

Re-enter SIR CHARLES, *who has overhead the last few lines,* L.

SIR CHARLES. Yes, that's the principle, Mr. Bunkum (*bell rings at outer door.* CHARLOTTE *goes to window, then returns* to JANE).

CHARLOTTE. There's the butcher's boy. He threatened yesterday that he would come to-day, and not leave without the money. He's so strong, and so shiny (JANE *and* CHARLOTTE *move towards door*).

SIR CHARLES. They all are—it's suet and fresh air. Shall I come and assist (*Kicks out his foot.*)

JANE. No, no. We shall soon be back.

Exeunt JANE *and* CHARLOTTE, R.

SIR CHARLES (*taking a bottle of champagne from basket and proceeding to open it*). This is friendly, Mr. Bunkum. Take a glass of wine (*Pours out glass of wine, and offers to* BUNKUM.)

BUNKUM. Wall; you seem to make pretty free with this room (*takes the glass cautiously*).

SIR CHARLES (*pouring out glass of wine for himself and drinking it*). Yes, I suppose I do, seeing whose room it is. I, think you'll like this fiz, though it *is* Blackfriars—real "Blue Lion," I assure you.

BUNKUM (*looking round room*). This is your room— is it? A. few minutes ago it was somebody else's.

SIR CHARLES. I see you have not heard that poor Miss Britain is in difficulties.

BUNKUM. Yes, I hev.

SIR CHARLES. And that, as she can't afford to occupy her ground floor any longer Cupid has just taken it off her hands.

BUNKUM (*sarcastically*). Wall no, that I hadn't heard.

SIR, CHARLES. Cupid has already begun, as you perceive, his flitting (*pointing to Needle*). Take another glass. Now that you and he are on different floors, he hopes you will be friends.

BUNKUM (*drinking the wine*). And what hev the floors to dew with Cupid's friendship, anyhow?

SIR CHARLES. Well, to be quite candid, he thought that, for people in the same line, your *keyholes* were too near!

BUNKUM. Oh! Cupid's an inventor, is he?

SIR CHARLES. Yes ; having, at last, got quite ready for the Patent Office the model of his Patent Walking Advertising Obelisk, and judging—*inferring*—that even if you *should* have hit upon the same idea (BUNKUM *begins to rise involuntarily from his chair*), your model would (BUNKUM *stands up*), owing to your modeller being ill in Paris, not he ready for a week (BUNKUM *throws down wine-glass, exclaims "Damnation " and walks towards Needle, while* ICHABOD *walks about, saying, "Keyhole, keyhole"*)—having *inferred* this, Cupid thought the convenient time had come (*he coolly takes up carving-knife from floor, and slowly sharpens it on the poker*) for him to quit a too close proximity to a professional American pirate. BUNKUM *springs round, pulls out his bowie-knife, while* SIR CHARLES *keeps coolly sharpening the carving-knife or poker, and* ICHABOD *keeps walking about displaying advertisements, and saying,* "Keyhole."

BUNKUM (*putting up bowie knife, but* SIR CHARLES *continues business with his*). Cuss that keyhole. I came across the river for quiet and secrecy, and I find *you*! I spotted you for the smartest man in this darned island. When I was makin' the drawing I watched you sharp; when I talked it over with the French modeller it wasn't much above a whisper; but I forgot the cussed keyhole till it was too late, and I found yours was stopped with plaster of Paris.

SIR CHARLES (*aside*). To keep out the draught (*to* BUNKUM). What a singular omission. You should have noticed Cupid's. A god, who stops his keyhole with plaster of Paris understands the article keyhole in *all* its functions.

BUNKUM (*looking at* SIR CHARLES *with vexation mixed with admiration*). Wall, you *air* smart, Cupid! You air that! The man as chops down CINCINNATUS BUNKUM *hes* to be smart. And the man as can copy a drawin' through a keyhole *is* smart. But what air yew whetting that knife for?

SIR CHARLES. Simply because I'm going to pitch into that chicken (*pointing to chicken*), and I thought it seemed blunt at the point, and I hate carving with a blunt knife (*strikes panel of door, L., with knife, piercing the panel through, and then with-drawing it with great velocity*).

BUNKUM. Cupid's a strong carver anyhow. You're right in sayin' we ought to be friends. Now, what's your game? Is it takin' out the patent, or is it bein' bought off? If it's bein' bought off, I'm open to treat; for nobody can't work *that* patent only me; but, mind, draw it mild, I ain't a goin' to be eel-skinned and thawed up, nohow.

SIR CHARLES. Perhaps I had better dismiss my man, and then we can talk at leisure (*goes to Needle and releases* ICHABOD. *To* ICHABOD). I think you can escape now while I hold him in conversation.

ICHABOD. Thank you, sir, for all your kindness. He's a dangerous customer and no mistake, but the carvin' knife scared him! I'll go and find my father, and tell him the people are all mad, and I'll go and tell the sheriff it's of no use his putting executions into madhouses.

SIR CHARLES. I should if I were you. Good-bye.

Exit ICHABOD.

SIR CHARLES. Sit down, Mr. Bunkum. (*They sit down at the table.*) Nobody can work the patent, only you, Mr. Bunkum! That sounds like vanity. I know Cupid's working *his* pretty well. A month ago he hadn't a shilling, and now he's got enough to take these rooms, besides paying off Miss Britain's mortgage money, clearing out the bailiffs, and stopping the sale.

BUNKUM. Why, your patent isn't out yet.

SIR CHARLES. Mr. Bunkum, as a smart man, you are falling in my estimation every moment. Cupid didn't wait for the patent to be out, but got a month's advance of advertisement money for a forthcoming mysterious invention without a name.

BUNKUM. You air jest now sharpening the razor rather *too* fine, Cupid. What you've jest told me *is—a—*damned lie. The British public *will* stand a good deal, but they won't stand that—I've tried it. They won't stand the pig in the poke, *no-how.*

SIR CHARLES. The public *do* stand it from Cupid, however, and, what's more, the advertising agents allow him a fixed income for Needle fees before they've seen the Needle.

BUNKUM (*throwing himself back in his chair*). Ha! ha! It ain't often as anybody fetches a laugh like

that out of Cincinnatus Bunkum. But *yew* can—
ha, ha! ha, ha! Wall, it's ridiculous.

SIR CHARLES. Is it? You seem amused (*looking off*).
Here's one of Cupid's employees coming back at
the very nick of time, to save his character both for
smartness and for voracity.

BUNKUM (*looking off*). One of your *employees*?
What! that old woman with the umbrella and the
basket—ha! ha! ha! Wall, I like yew; yew *can* make
me laugh, yew *can*.

SIR CHARLES. One of Cupid's employees. Love is
the only true wisdom. The little god knows that
the best of all ways in this country to make money
is to base your speculations on philanthropy.

BUNKUM. Wall, that's true, anyhow.

SIR CHARLES. So Cupid has turned all the widows
in the neighbourhood into canvassers on com-
mission; and the way they go from tradesmen to
tradesmen, canvassing for advertisements, with
special instructions as to cash in advance, is another instance—if one were needed of the lamentable
waste of material in this country. As a touching
proof that they *are* industrious British widows,
they always receive the subscriptions in that
old-fashioned and, alas! obsolete British purse—
the worsted stocking.

BUNKUM. Wall, yew *can* make me laugh, yew can ha! ha!

SIR CHARLES. I assure you the stocking is a *great* hit. Sentiment is a great factor in money-getting.

BUNKUM. Wall, Cupid is the most brilliant liar this side Kentucky, any how.

Enter MRS. THROGMORTON, *with basket.*

MRS. THROGMORTON (*handing* SIR CHARLES *ten pounds*). Here's the ten pounds separate. I'll give you the Needle fee, fust, sir.

BUNKUM (*starting up*). WHAT!—what did you say that money was for, ma'am.

MRS. THROGMORTON. Lud, how you startle me! That's the Needle fee, of course.

BUNKUM. The Needle fee! and what's the Needle fee for, ma'am?

MRS. THROGMORTON. The Needle fee! Why, that's for the advertisements.

BUNKUM (*sinking down in his chair*). Wall, I am chopped down. Yes, yes, I *am* chopped down, this time!

Re-enter JANE, R, *with bill of postponement in her hand, advancing to table.*

JANE. Mr. Bright, see this! (*stands amazed at the sight of* MRS. THROGMORTON).

MRS. THROGMORTON (*to* SIR CHARLES). And here's the stocking, sir (*she empties the stocking on the table, and the contents, gold, silver, and copper, roll about* BUNKUM'S *and* JANE'S *hands*).

SIR CHARLES. And how much other money have you brought me?

MRS. THROGMORTON. Three hundred pounds fifteen shillings and sixpence.

SIR CHARLES. (*in a patronising tone*). Very fair (*patting her on the back*), very fair.

MRS. THROGMORTON (*looking at him in amazement, aside*). What a pleasant gentleman this is! He seems to have taken quite a fancy to me! (*Sees* JANE, *aside.*) Why, here's Jane! must git her away, and buy the property on her, before she knows anything' about this.

BUNKUM. You air the smartest man!—But it *must* be a plant. (*To* MRS. THROGMORTON) Then this gentleman sends you about a good deal, does he? Where hev you been to-day for him?

MRS. THROGMORTON. Well, let me see! First I
went to the cabman, and gave him the letter for
Lady Threadneedle, tell in' her that her money was
ready for her as soon as she liked to have it. And
then I went to the printing-office with this gentleman's letter to the printer, tellin' him to print the
bills about the postponement of the sale (*she goes
to* JANE, *who has retired in amazement to the back,
and converses energetically with her*).

SIR CHARLES (*to* BUNKUM). The fact is, Cupid
makes these old girls generally useful. They do all
his errands.

BUNKUM (*looking at him, dreamily*). Wall, Cupid is
the smartest man in all creation.

SIR CHARLES (*rising*). Well, Mr. Bunkum, I suppose we've not much more to say to each other.

BUNKUM. Wall, yes, I guess we hey. Fust of all (*holding out his hand*), I beg your pardon for giving you
the lie jest now. Second, I've been tryin' all my life
tew find a man smart enough tew jine me in business. I couldn't find him, but if he's to *be* found, I
think he's the owner of that Needle (*pointing to it*).

SIR CHARLES. Really, you are too kind.

BUNKUM. A man as can pirate a design through a keyhole, and work it out, and be ready for patentin' a week afore *me*, to say nothin' of gittin' John Bull to pay for advertising in a scheme without a name, and gittin' the advertisin' agent to pay a Needle fee afore ever the Needle's made, seems to me exactly the man I've been lookin' for. Wull you jine me? Don't you think it seems a pity we should be parted?

SIR CHARLES. But wouldn't the name of the firm look rather queer, Bunkum, Honour Bright, and Co.

BUNKUM. Don't see that at all. In the commarcial world Bunkum and Honour Bright are gittin' to hey pretty much the same kind of sound, I guess.

SIR CHARLES. Well, if you don't mind the incongruity, I don't. We'll join our fortunes. You've got your cheque-book with you I noticed; sit down (*beckons him to a table and arranges paper, pens, and ink before him*).

BUNKUM. What's the cheque-book got to do with it anyhow?

SIR CHARLES. Really, Mr. Bunkum, we start badly, I fear. *I* bring in that (*pointing to Needle*), worth at least £10,000; *you* write me a cheque for, let us say, £2,000, in part of the cash capital, to be afterwards settled, which *you* bring in to balance *my* Needle.

BUNKUM (*looking at him suspiciously and yet admiringly*). Wall, you *air* smart! (*Aside*) The patent *is* worth a long figure; but, as a partner, your figure's longer (*sits down and writes.* SIR CHARLES *looks over his shoulder*).

SIR CHARLES. No, put it thus: Pay to Honour Bright, Esq., £2,000 as a premium for going into partnership with him. (*Aside*) Then, when the explanation about the model comes, I shan't get into any real trouble about that (BUNKUM *throws himself back in his chair and reflects; then he looks at* SIR CHARLES *scrutinisingly, and signs*).

SIR CHARLES. No, don't cross it. I shall cash it at once.

JANE (*advancing to* SIR CHARLES). Mr. Bright, do tell me what makes this extraordinary change in my aunt. She puzzles me; she's so anxious now to buy this house.

SIR CHARLES. Don't strike a bargain with her by any means; don't do anything without me.

JANE. That I certainly will not; for you are, indeed, a treasure.

SIR CHARLES. Is the little god winning?

JANE. He has won. SIR CHARLES (*advancing to her with the cheque which he has taken from* BUNKUM). Would you send Charlotte to cash this at once?

JANE (*looking at cheque*). Mr. Bunkum! (*and then looking at* SIR CHARLES). Wonderful man!

Exit R, *followed by* MRS. THROGMORTON.

BUNKUM (*who has been watching them*). Wall, partner, and what does all that whisperin' mean? Is that a *very* good bit o' business?

SIR CHARLES (mounting chair and pinning postponement poster over sale bill). Oh! this is a separate account. Our partnership is patents only.

BUNKUM. No! (*Observing postponement poster*) I don't see that. It's a general partnership. There's no deed between us yet, but, honour——

SIR CHARLES. Among thieves, you were going to say (*descending*). But this is my best spec, and has nothing to do with the partnership. But tell you what you *shall* do, if you like you shall buy a *third* of my interest at a sum fixed—paying down, of course.

BUNKUM. Wall! (*suspiciously*) what is it?

SIR CHARLES. Read that paragraph (*hands him "Blackfriars Gazette"*).

BUNKUM (*starting up*). Site of the Needle—why, the Compensation money!

SIR CHARLES (*looking at him*). Yes, I know.

BUNKUM (*regaining his coolness*). Now, I know why you sent the notices to Lady Throgmorton. You are the—— You're buying it before anybody knows, of course.

SIR CHARLES. Of course. You don't suppose I should have waited till they do know.

BUNKUM. Wall; now—what will you let me in at?

SIR CHARLES. For a third, you know; no more than a third. Well, I'm not a greedy man. Make the cheque for £1,500.

BUNKUM (*looking at him, and then at poster, and then at paragraph*). No, I'm damned if I'll touch *this*, anyhow.

SIR CHARLES. Now, come, that's kind of you. It would *not* have been fair. I did really consider the partnership special (BUNKUM *sits down, writes cheque, and hands it to* SIR CHARLES).

SIR CHARLES (*refusing to take it*). No, no. You declined.

BUNKUM. Yes; business is business. You've been too smart for *me*. But I guess I'm a little too smart for *you*, this time (*lays down cheque on table*).

SIR CHARLES (*taking it up and putting it in his pocket*). Yes, you're too smart for me this time, Mr. Bunkum.

BUNKUM. If you're going to cash this at once, too, I must just go and see what my balance is (*going*). Let me ask you one question, partner. What *are* you—by profession?

SIR CHARLES. An English baronet.

BUNKUM (*in amazement*). One of the British upper ten? Why, I thought they were all Dundrearys, all fools.

SIR CHARLES. Not when inspired by Cupid, Mr. Bunkum.

Exit BUNKUM, L.

Enter JANE, *followed by* CHARLOTTE.

JANE. The cheque is cashed; here's the money (*lays it on table*). But what does this change mean in my aunt? She's turned into an angel.

161

SIR CHARLES. All Cupid! She's brought you this money—just to go on with (*pointing to money on table*). And look here! I'm so sorry to trouble you again; but this other cheque would you kindly get that cashed, too, and at once? the branch-bank will be closed shortly.

JANE (*looking at cheque*). Bunkum! Why, what can all this mean?

SIR CHARLES. Simply that Cupid has won (JANE *hands cheque to* CHARLOTTE, *who goes out*). When Fortune is very blind and won't give Cupid a turn, Cupid considers it only fair to turn the wheel for her. Follow my cue in all I say and do (*enters Needle*).

Re-enter MRS. THROGMORTON, R.

MRS. THROGMORTON. Why, where's the Govr'ement gentleman (*looks at* SIR CHARLES' *face in Needle*). Bless me, how the Prime Minister has altered. (*Sees postponement poster*) Why that'll bring everybody to bid against me. (*Approaching* JANE *and whispering*.) My dear, I'm a goin' to stan' your friend, for the sake of your poor mother. How much shall I give you for the house, jest to keep it away from that nasty old Lady Threadneedle, and keep it in the family?

Re-enter CHARLOTTE, *followed by* LADY THREADNEEDLE *and* FOOTMAN, R.

CHARLOTTE. Lady Threadneedle.

Exit R.

LADY THREADNEEDLE (*to* JANE). Why, what does this mean, Miss Britain? Who gave orders for this postponement? (JANE *hands her newspaper, and points to paragraph*).

LADY THREADNEEDLE (*starting as she reads*). Impossible! And yet the site is so very unsuitable that it must be true (*turns round and sees Needle, but not the face*). And I declare! (*looks at it through her eye-glass*) what does this mean? A model of the Needle here. (*Aside*) If this news is true, what money will be made! (*To* JANE) I expect my solicitor here shortly. I shall be quite willing to buy the house and stand your friend.

SIR CHARLES (*from Needle*). Always look well after a purchaser that buys to stand your friend (*turns round, again so that the face is not seen*).

LADY THREADNEEDLE (*looking round in amazement through her eye-glass, to* MRS. THROGMORTON). What did you say?

MRS. THROGMORTON. What did you say?

LADY THREADNEEDLE (*aside*). This is done to drive me off but I'll buy it if it is to be bought.

MRS. THROGMORTON (*coming up to* JANE). My dear, the party to stand your friend is your own aunt by the mother's side—the clussest of all aunts, for father's-side-aunts are *allus* disagreeable (LADY THREADNEEDLE *looks at* THROGMORTON *through her eye-glass*).

SIR CHARLES (*from Needle*). Who is this person?

MRS. THROGMORTON (*turning round upon* LADY THREAD-NEEDLE). Person! No more a person than you. Person, indeed!

LADY THREADNEEDLE (*losing her temper*). Do you know whom you are addressing?

MRS. THROGMORTON. Oh, yes! You're my Lady Threadneedle. You make money in a big way; I make money in a little way. You do it genteel; I do it low.

SIR CHARLES (*from Needle*). Wholesale rogue and retail.

LADY THREADNEEDLE (*looking round, and then at* MRS. THROGMORTON). What an extraordinary person! But I'm not going to be befooled by a vulgar old ventriloquist.

MRS. THROGMORTON. What do you mean by callin' me a rogue? If you come to that, there ain't much difference between you and me, except the heye-glass and the lady-ship.

LADY THREADNEEDLE (*becoming very angry*). You false woman! You know it was *you* who called *me* a rogue.

MRS. THROGMORTON. Oh, what a lie!

SIR CHARLES (*from Needle*). I'll have you locked up.

MRS. THROGMORTON (*turning upon* LADY THREADNEEDLE *in great wrath*). *You* have *me* locked up!

LADY THREADNEEDLE. You know I didn't say so, you bad, designing woman! You know you said it yourself—you—you—you—you wicked old—old—ventriloquist!

MRS. THROGMORTON. *You* have me locked up! There's a law for the rich and a law for the poor, else *you'd* stand a chance of being locked up yourself for comin' here and trying to cheat a poor, unpertected young female and her poor old aunt—trying to make us sell our family estate for a few hundreds when it's worth so many thousands (*turning to* JANE). I didn't mean all that, my dear, only I must shut her up.

SIR CHARLES (*from Needle*). Don't quarrel! Both in the same boat, you know. If Throgmorton's a rogue, so is Threadneedle.

LADY THREADNEEDLE. There you are again! You want to drive me away by your low insults, but you'll find I'm not to be beaten.

MRS. THROGMORTON. There *you* are again—callin' me a rogue. But you'll find *I* ain't to be beaten. I'll buy it over your head if it busts me! Do you let me come and speak to my niece (*pushing* LADY THREADNEEDLE *violently*). My dear, I'll give you nine hundred pounds for the house.

LADY THREADNEEDLE. Miss Britain, I'll give you nine hundred and fifty pounds for the house.

Re-enter CHARLOTTE, *with cash*, R.

CHARLOTTE. Here's all Blackfriars coming, with posters in their hands.

MRS. THROGMORTON (*very excitedly, and pulling* LADY THREAD-NEEDLE'S *shawl*). Don't let the family be cheated, Jane. It's worth more, my dear; it's worth a good deal more—no, not a good deal more a little *more*. I'll give you ten hundred (*as* LADY THREADNEEDLE *is about to speak,* MRS. THROGMORTON *flies upon her, and they fight*).

SIR CHARLES (*from Needle*). Don't fight, ladies! As the property is going to the highest bidder, I will mount the table, become my own auctioneer, and play Mammon myself! (LADY THREADNEEDLE *and* MRS. THROGMORTON *both turn round*).

JANE. As the property is going to the highest bidder, I will mount the table, become my own auctioneer, and play Mammon myself (*mounting table. Aside*). This is too charming. I will let him see how I can enter into his glorious spirit of fun

(CHARLOTTE, *by* JANE'S *directions, hands her up a chair and stand, and a brush, to use as an auctioneer's* hammer).

MRS. THROGMORTON (*rushing up to table*). No nonsense, Jane; no tomfoolery, Jane. Don't let it go out of the family. I'll give you another hundred—and that's the last I *will* give.

JANE (*imitating the auctioneer*). Thank you, aunt; thank you. Another hundred bid for this fine site—going at eleven hundred, if no advance—going at eleven hundred.

LADY THREADNEEDLE. I'll give you another twenty pounds.

SIR CHARLES (*from Needle*). And that's the last I will give.

JANE. Thank you, my lady. Eleven hundred and twenty pounds bid for this noble site—going at eleven hundred and twenty—going at eleven hundred and twenty—going, going, going!

MRS. THROGMORTON. Eleven hundred and thirty, and that's all I will give.

SIR CHARLES (*from Needle*). Eleven hundred and forty.

MRS. THROGMORTON (*turning to* LADY THREADNEEDLE). What do you mean by tellin' such a lie as sayin' you wouldn't bid no higher, and go and bid directly—cheatin' me out of a ten-pound note.

LADY THREADNEEDLE. I didn't say so you know I didn't (*advances to table to bid, when MRS. THROGMORTON seizes her bonnet, and tears it off. LADY THREADNEEDLE strikes her—a scuffle ensues*).

JANE (*hilariously imitating auctioneer*). Now, Lady Threadneedle, I am quite ready to take your bid! May I say another twenty? Thank you, another twenty. It stands at Lady Threadneedle at eleven hundred and sixty. Going at eleven hundred and sixty if no advance; going, going, going at eleven hundred and sixty, going at eleven hundred and sixty, this valuable property which is so shortly to become famous as the site of Cleopatra's Needle, a model of which you see before you. Going at eleven hundred and sixty if no advance. Now, aunty dear, don't let it go out of the family at such an absurd sum. Going once, going twice, going.

MRS. THROGMORTON (*shrieking*). Another twenty, Jane; knock it down.

JANE. Thank you, aunty dear, another twenty; eleven hundred pounds and eighty bid for this noble site shortly to become so famous.

MRS. THROGMORTON. Knock it down.

JANE. Not yet, aunty dear, not yet. We mustn't let the property be thrown away at such a figure.

Enter MISS JOHNSON, R. *with a copy of the newspaper in her hand and poster.*

Ah, here comes another bidder! My first-floor front—Miss Johnson. So sorry I cannot take your bid, Miss Johnson, but deposit must be paid down, and, without wishing to be indelicate—it must still stand at Mrs. Throgmorton at eleven hundred and eighty pounds, and it's going at eleven hundred and eighty pounds. Going at eleven hundred and eighty pounds, if no advance.

MISS JOHNSON. Eleven hundred and ninety.

JANE. Now, really, Miss Johnson, if I could only take your bid, I should really be delighted to see you make a bargain that would enable you to *leave* a first-floor front under which smoulders, like a female volcano, a speculator who loses.

Enter MR. ZERUBBABEL SMITH, R., with poster and newspaper in his hand.

Going at eleven hundred and ninety pounds, if no advance. (*Perceiving* Z. SMITH.) Now, I declare, here's another estimable bidder, whose bid, I regret to say, I cannot possibly take.

Z. SMITH. I assure you my bid may be taken with perfect safety. As secretary of the Self-Abnegation Building Society, I have an unlimited command of funds.

JANE. But, my dear Mr. Smith, it is not your own.

Z. SMITH. That doesn't at all signify, I assure you.

JANE. Mr. Smith, Mr. Smith, speculation is the great vice of this age.

Enter CINCINNATUS BUNKUM R, *followed by a number of tradesmen in their aprons, who rush in excitedly, with newspapers and posters in their hands. Bidding goes on furiously from all parties. Angry altercations ensue between all of them.*

JANE (*at the top of her voice*). Going at fifteen hundred and ninety pounds; going at fifteen hundred and ninety pounds going, if no advance, going! going! going! (*More tradesmen rush in, bidding furiously; great uproar.*) Here they come, the brewer, the baker, the candlestick-maker (*nodding to various bidders*). Thank you, thank you. The property now stands at two thousand and eighty pounds. Going at two thousand and eighty pounds, if no advance—going! going! going! What! all done? All done? Well, then, it's Lady Threadneedle's, after all (*knocks down hammer*). Accept, ladies and gentlemen, my thanks on behalf of myself, no less than Mr. Mammon, whom I represent, for your patronage and courtesy, and the very spirited way in which you have been bidding up (*descends*).

SIR CHARLES (*coming from Needle*). By Jove! that's the finest girl in London. If she'll have me, I'll marry her to-morrow, and have old Mother Throgmorton for an aunt. (*He goes up to her*) Miss Britain, I can't say how much I admire you as an auctioneer. (*Aside.*) (Was there ever such a piquante, brilliant, plucky—No! I'm damned if ever there was.) Miss Britain I want to speak to you (*they converse apart*).

Enter MR. DIDDLUM, R, *with blue bag, in great haste.*

LADY THREADNEEDLE (*rushing up to him*). I've bought the site of Cleopatra's Needle.

DIDDLUM. There must be some mistake.

LADY THREADNEEDLE. No, no. Write out a cheque for the money. Never mind about the formalities till afterwards. Give her the cheque (*Diddlum sits down, and writes cheque*).

DIDDLUM (*coming up to* JANE). Here is the cheque, Miss Britain (JANE *takes cheque*).

NEWSPAPER BOY (*outside*). *Echo! Echo! Echo!* Fifth edish-on. Site of Cleopatra's Needle. (*There is a general rush to the door, and "Echo" boy is pulled in.*)

BUNKUM (reading "Echo" aloud). The authorities have at last decided that the site of Cleopatra's Needle is to be either on the Embankment, or in Parliament-square, or on Primrose-hill, or somewhere else (*There is a general uproar and laughter, and cries of "A hoax!"*).

DIDDLUM (*making towards* LADY THREAD-NEEDLE). Fraud, deceit. We have been embezzled out of our deposit money. (*Turning round.*) Who has done this Where's the scoundrel Where's the scoundrel?

172

BUNKUM. There he is, the pirate of that Sphinx. Damn him! The smartest man in all creation.

LADY THREADNEEDLE (*going up to* SIR CHARLES). Who are you that have cheated me? (*recognises him*) Sir Charles Larkie!

SIR CHARLES. Yes, and the purchaser of the site of Cleopatra's Needle. The auctioneer took the wrong bid. It should have been knocked down to me (*takes cheque from* JANE *and hands it to* DIDDLUM). Allow me, Lady Threadneedle, to present to you my future wife. And as Cleopatra's Needle has brought about the match, I propose we have the Needle Dance.

Dance.

CURTAIN.

APPENDIXES

ANOYMOUS REVIEW OF "A VISION OF LOVE REVEALED IN SLEEP"

(First published in *The Athenæum,*
25th of March 1871)

IT is always difficult for the reader to assure himself that he understands all that an allegory means, or is intended by the author to mean. We feel, therefore, some hesitation in interpreting Mr. Simeon Solomon's pretty, though not very powerful myth. If we are not mistaken, it is a sort of palinode to Love; not such a palinode as Socrates pronounces in Plato's "Phaedrus", when he conceives that he has spoken profanely of the Divinity, but such as might be pronounced by the ἀκόλαστος of the Platonic apologue when he came to repent of his youthful errors, or by one of "the company with heated eyes," in the Poet-Laureate's "Vision of Sin," who had succeeded in breaking away from his fellows ere it grew too late. The palinode, if such it is, describes in mystic and poetical prose the stages

177

through which the "child of sin" passes from the time when Love stands before him—"dethroned and captive, bound and wounded, bereft of the natural light of his presence; his wings drooping, broken, and torn; his hands made fast to the barren and leafless tree; the myrtles upon his brow withered and falling; and upon that heart, from whose living depths should proceed the voice of the revolving spheres, a wound flowing with blood, which changed into roses of divinest odour as it fell,"—until "the Very Love, the Divine Type of Absolute Beauty, primeval and eternal, compact of the white flame of youth, burning in unutterable perfection," is glorified in a Beatific Vision. Such is the most natural interpretation of the allegory; but we cannot speak with certainty upon the subject. Myths and apologues, like signs and prophecies, will bear many meanings; and we cannot be sure that the Apotheosis of Love does not figure the development of morality, the revival of science and learning, or a dozen other things. Mr. Solomon writes in that epithetical, somewhat affected style, which writers of apologues usually adopt. His English is careful and ornate, but lacks, in our opinion, force and originality. We have already hinted that the myth itself, though pretty, is wanting in substance. The volume, which is luxuriously printed, contains a photograph of a picture by the author, which exemplifies at once his merits and his defects. As a painter, Mr. Solomon seems to possess a genuine love of the beautiful. The same appreciation of beauty of form shows itself in his poetical prose; but he should remember that prettiness of expression is no sufficient reason for the existence of a book, even if (and this we doubt) mere beauty of form is a sufficient reason for the existence of a picture. We wish that Mr. Solomon had given us the whole of his allegory in the pictorial shape in which he has already represented one or two scenes of it. It may be, of course, that he intends the "Vision of Love" merely as a key to a series of pictures. We sincerely hope that it is so, and that all will be as beautiful as the picture reproduced in the "Portfolio," with the title, "Until the day break and the shadows flee away."

REVIEW OF "A VISION OF LOVE REVEALED IN SLEEP"

by J. A. Symonds

(First published in *The Academy*, 1ˢᵗ of April 1871)

WE have every reason to congratulate ourselves when the genius of a distinguished artist finds a double channel for its self-expression—when a poet can furnish us with illustrations of his poems copied from the very visions which inspired them, or when a painter is able to tell us in words what he means to convey to our imaginations by the forms and colours of his pictures. Mr. Solomon's prose poem is a key to the meaning of his drawings. It lays bare the hidden purpose of the artist, and enables us to connect picture with picture in a perfectly intelligible series. Those who are familiar with his sketches or with the photographs which have been taken from them will recognise the perfect unity of style which marks the vision and the outlined forms. Those again who can appreciate the delicate and subtle key of colour used by the painter in his finished pictures will trace the same harmonies of hue in many of the descriptions of the vision, for instance in the vestments tinted "the heart of an opal" and "like a flame seen through water" of the final scene.

As its name implies, this prose poem has for its subject Love. The mystery of Love is here displayed as in a pageant to the dreaming spirit of the poet by his soul conceived as an external and superior power. It is not therefore without good reason that the single illustration with which the book is adorned should represent the Soul and the Novice: in the same way, if a medieval artist had designed one woodcut for the *Divine Comedy* he would probably have drawn Dante with Virgil or with Beatrice as his initiator in the mysteries of the spiritual world.

The Love of Mr. Solomon's *Vision* is quite distinct and unconventional. He is unlike the "bitter sweet impracticable wild Beast" who bent Sappho's soul as "storms break oaks upon the mountains." He is unlike the blacksmith of Anacreon's Mythus, who forged the soul upon an anvil and then plunged it in a wintry stream. Nor again has he anything in common with the beautiful winged boy of Praxiteles, or with the runaway of Moschus. The parrot-winged fire-faced child of Arabian fancy belongs to another race and lineage. So does that champion of chivalrous love beheld in vision by Pierre Vidal, who rode a snow-white horse and had the face and limbs of a young knight, followed by the damsels Modesty and Mercy, and by Loyalty for squire. Nor, again, is the Love of this new

Mythus to be found upon the pages of the *Vita Nuova*. The pilgrim who met Dante on the Way of Sighs, the grave-faced and inexorable youth who sat by his bed-side and wept, and communed with him, and was sweet and stem, has more perhaps in common with the Love of Mr. Solomon's *Vision* than any other. But he is not the same. In truth, the originality of any po-etical or pictorial Mythus, such as is embodied in this vision and in the series of Mr. Solomon's drawings, consists in its creator having viewed an old problem with new eyes, and communicated to the object some of the qualities of his own soul and of the age in which he lives. This, in our opinion, Mr. Solomon has done with eminent and unmistakable distinctness. His Love is not classical, not medieval, not Oriental; but it has a touch of all these qualities—the pure perfection of the classic form, the allegorical mysticism and pensive grace of the middle age, and the indescribable per-fume of Orientalism, which, by the way, finds a more than usually definite expression in the last scene of this vision. Added to these general qualities we trace in this spirit of love a vague yet intense yearning, a *Sebnsucht*, which belongs to music and is essentially modem. If, finally, we seek that characteristic which is most truly peculiar to the poet himself, we find it to be a certain Biblical solemnity of spiritual sense inbreathed, as Milton phrases it, into the forms of art.

It savours somewhat of Philistinism to question the details of a vision and to expect an exact meaning in all the figures of so pictorial a work of imagination as this of Mr. Solomon's. Yet we may call attention to the subtlety by which he has divided the soul of the seer from the man himself, and has made that soul with purged and disembodied vision act as the hierophant of a revelation which the man in his completeness would have been incapable of discerning. Other poets have chosen some guide, like the Sibyl of Virgil or the Beatrice of Dante or the Angel of the Apocalypse, for their illuminator. Mr. Solomon has proved the modem quality of his genius by the selection of no other power than that of the indwelling soul of man. The first words of the soul upon the pathway of initiation are:—

"Thou hast looked upon me, and thou knowest me well, for in me thou but seest thyself, not hidden and obscure by the cruel veil of the flesh. I am come forth of thee for thy well-doing."

After this preface the soul leads forth the seer to a place where Memory abides; then showing him simple Pleasure in the figure of a woman:

"Looking upon her, I saw that she was good, but I knew that there was that about her that left me not content; she was like as sweet notes heard once and lost for ever."

Then they come to the station of Love bruised and bound; where also Passion is revealed as "she who had wounded and had sought to slay Love, but who, in her turn, was grievously wounded and tormented in strange, self-devised ways." Passing from this place, they reach "him who had done battle with Love, Death, who would love us did he dare, whom we would love did we dare." Parenthetically it may be said that one of the most beautiful and subtly finished portions of this *Vision* is that in which Death is described. Divine Charity bringing Sleep to earth. Time holding stricken Love within his arms, and Night and Dawn and Day, and the Spirit of Dreams in sleep, are all seen in the successions of the mystery. Till at length, after a space of time and after due lustrations and equipment in the robes of purity, insight is granted to the seer into the holiest of Holies, where Love himself, no longer afflicted and dethroned, but in his glory and his power, is displayed. Thus lightly and vaguely to indicate a few scenes of the *Vision* is all that a critic can attempt. To read the inner meaning of the mystery—to decide whether Love wounded by Passion upon earth, abandoned to oblivion, put out of sight and overgrown by weeds and briars of this mortal life, is revealed in his full splendour at the gates of Death, or Death's twin-brother Sleep—must be left to the judgment of the readers of the pages of this book.

It is enough once more to point out the subtle harmony which subsists between the poetic and the pictorial faculties of the artist's genius. Those who desire a comment on the figured allegories of Mr. Solomon will find it in his *Vision*; those who wish to see his vision as he saw it with their very eyes have only to turn to his drawings for full and ample illustration. The frontispiece of the book is itself a good example of the painter's style, at the same time that it sets forth the relation he desires to establish between the seer and the soul.

If any definite criticism should be added to this account of Mr. Solomon's *Vision*, it must be that there is a certain vagueness in the succession of the scenes, and that his literary style, while it shares the delicacy and peculiar flavour of his pictures, has somewhat also of their profuse perfume and languor. To lay stress on these points would be ungrateful. We should rather be thankful that such an artist as Mr. Solomon has found a voice so dear and sweet as that which may be listened to in this narration of his Apocalypse of Love.

—J. A. SYMONDS

SIMEON SOLOMON: NOTES ON HIS "VISION OF LOVE" AND OTHER STUDIES

by Algernon Charles Swinburne

(First published in *The Dark Blue*, 1ˢᵗ of July 1871)

IF it may be said with perfect accuracy that in all plastic art, whether the language chosen be of words or forms, of sounds or colours, beauty is the only truth, and nothing not beautiful is true; yet this axiom of a great living artist and critic must not be so construed as to imply forgetfulness of the manifold and multi-form nature of beauty. To one interpreter the terror or the pity of it, the shadow or the splendour, will appear as its main aspect, as that which gives him his fittest material for work or speech, the substance most plia-ble to his spirit, the form most suggestive to his hand; to another its simplicity or its mystery, its community or its specialty of gifts. Each servant serves under the compulsion of his own charm; each spirit has its own chain. Upon men in whom there is, so to speak, a compound genius, an intermixture of spiritual forces, a confluence of separate yet conspiring influences, diverse in source yet congruous in result—upon men in whose eyes the boundary lines of the several conterminous arts appear less as lines of mere distinction than as lines of mutual alliance—the impression of the mystery in all beauty, and in all defects that fall short of it, and in all excesses that overbear it, is likely to have a special hold. The subtle interfusion of art with art, of sound with form, of vocal words with silent colours, is as perceptible to the sense and as inexplicable to the understanding of such men as the interfusion of spirit with flesh is to all men in common; and in fact when perceived of no less significance than this, but rather a part and complement of the same truth. One of such artists, and at once recognisable as such, is Mr. Simeon Solomon. There is not, for instance, more of the painter's art in the verse of Keats than of the musician's in Solomon's designs. As surely as the mystery of beauty—a mystery "most glad and sad," as Chaucer says of a woman's mouth—was done into colour of verse for ever unsurpassable in the odes "To a Nightingale" and on "Melancholy," so is the same secret wrought into perfect music of outline by the painter. The "unheard melodies," which Keats, with a sense beyond the senses, perceived and enjoyed in the forms of his Grecian urn, vibrate in the forms of this artist's handiwork; and all their lines and colours,

> Not to the sensual ear, but more endeared,
> Pipe to the spirit ditties of no tone.

Since the first years of his very early and brilliant celebrity as a young artist of high imaginative power and promise, Mr. Solomon has been at work long enough to enable us to define at least certain salient and dominant points of his genius. It holds at once of east and west, of Greek and Hebrew. So much indeed does this fresh interfusion of influences give tone and shape to his imagination, that I have heard him likened on this ground to Heine, as a kindred Hellenist of the Hebrews. Grecian form and beauty divide the allegiance of his spirit with Hebraic shadow and majesty: depths of cloud unsearchable and summits unsurmountable of fire darken and lighten before the vision of a soul enamoured of soft light and clear water, of leaves and flowers and limbs more lovely than these. For no painter has more love of loveliness; but the fair forms of godhead and manhood which in ancient art are purely and merely beautiful rise again under his hand with the likeness on them of a new thing, the shadow of a new sense, the hint of a new meaning; their eyes have seen in sleep or waking, in substance or reflection, some change now past or passing or to come; their lips have tasted a new savour in the wine of life, one strange and alien to the vintage of old; they know of something beyond form and outside of speech. There is a questioning wonder in their faces, a fine joy and a faint sorrow, a trouble as of water stirred, a delight as of thirst appeased. Always, at feast or sacrifice, in chamber or in field, the air and carriage of their beauty has something in it of the strange:

hardly a figure but has some touch, though never so delicately slight, either of eagerness or of weariness, some note of expectancy or of satiety, some semblance of outlook or inlook: but prospective or introspective, an expression is there which is not pure Greek, a shade or tone of thought or feeling beyond Hellenic contemplation; whether it be oriental or modern in its origin, and derive from national or personal sources. This passionate sentiment of mystery seems at times to "o'erinform its tenement" of line and colour, and impress itself even to perplexity upon the sense of the spectator. The various studies, all full of subtleties and beauties definable and not definable, to which the artist has given for commentary the graceful mysticism of a symbolic rhapsody in prose, are also full to overflowing of such sentiment. Read by itself as a fragment of spiritual allegory, this written *Vision of Love revealed in Sleep* seems to want even that much coherence which is requisite to keep symbolic or allegoric art from absolute dissolution and collapse; that unity of outline and connection of purpose, that gradation of correlative parts and significance of corresponsive details, without which the whole aerial and tremulous fabric of symbolism must decompose into mere confusion of formless and fruitless chaos. Even allegory or prophecy must live and work by rule as well as by rapture; transparent it need not be, but it must be translucent. And translucent the fluctuating twilight of this rhapsody does become in time, with the light behind it of the designs; though at first it seems as hard to distinguish one incarnation of love or sleep or charity from the next following as to disentangle the wings and wheels of Ezekiel's cherubim, or to discover and deter mine the respective properties and qualities of Blake's "emanations" and "spectres." The style is soft, fluent, genuinely melodious; it has nothing of inflation or constraint. There is almost a superflux of images full of tender colour and subtle grace, which is sure to lead the writer into some danger of confusion and repetition; and in such vague and uncertain ground any such stumbling-blocks are likely to be especial rocks of offence to the feet of the traveller. Throughout the whole there is as it were a suffusion of music, a transpiration of light and sound, very delicately and surely sustained. There are thoughts and fragments of thoughts, fancies and fantastic symbols, sometimes of rare beauty and singular force; in this for instance, of Night as a mother watching Sleep her child, there is a greater height and sweetness of imagination than in any but the sweetest and highest poetic allegories. "And she, to whom all was as an open scroll, wept when she looked upon him whose heart was as the heart of a little child." The depth and tenderness of this conception of Night, omniscient with the conscience of all things wrought under her shadow, world-wide of sight and sway, and wise with all the world's wisdom, weeping for love over the innocence of her first-born, is great and perfect enough for the noblest verse of a poet. The same affluence and delicacy of emblems interwoven with every part of the allegory is kept up from the first dawn of memory to the last transfiguration of love. There is an exquisite touch in the first vision of Memory standing by the sea side with the shell held to her ear whose voice "unburied the dead cycles of the soul," with autumn leaves showered on head and breast, "and upon her raiment small flecks of foam had already dried;" this last emblem of the salt small foam-flecks, sharp and arid waifs of the unquiet sea of life, light and bitter strays of barren thought and remembrance with the freshness dried out of them, is beautiful and new. Dim and vague as the atmosphere of such work should be, this vision would be more significant, and not less suggestive of things hidden in secret places of spiritual reserve, if it had more body of drawing, more shape lines of thought and fixity of outline. Not that we would seek for solidity in shadow, or blame the beauty of luminous clouds for confusion of molten outlines; but even in cloud there is some law of form, some continuous harmony of line and mass, that only dissolves and changes "as a tune into a tune." To invigorate and support this fair frame of allegory there should be some clearer infusion of a purpose; there should be some thread of clearer connection, some filament, though never so slender, to link vision again to vision, some clue, "as subtle as Arachne's broken woof," to lead the reader's perception through the labyrinth of sounds and shapes. Each new revelation and change of aspect has beauty and meaning of its own; but even in a dream the steps of progress seem clearer than here, and the process from stage to stage of action or passion is ruled after some lawless law and irrational reason of its own. Such process as this at least we might hope to find even in the records of allegoric vision; in this mystery or tragedy of the passion of a divine sufferer "wounded in the house of his friends" and bleeding from the hands of men, those who follow the track of his pilgrimage might desire at least to be shown the stations of his cross. We miss the thread of union between the varying visions of love forsaken and shamed, wounded and forgotten; of guileless and soulless pleasure in its naked and melodious maidenhood, and passion that makes havoc of love, and after that even of itself also; of death and silence, and of sleep and time. Many of these have in them the sweetness and depth of good dreams, and much subtle and various beauty; and had we but some clue to the gradations of its course, we might thread our way through the Dædalian maze with a free sense of gratitude to the artificer whose cunning reared it to hide no monstrous thing, but one of divine likeness. It might have been well to issue with the text some further reproductions of the designs: those especially of the wounded Love from whose heart's blood the roses break into blossom, of Desire with body and raiment dishevelled and deformed from self-inflicted strokes, of Divine Charity bearing Sleep down to the dark earth among men that suffer, of Love upborne by the strong arms and wings of Time, of the spirit that watches in the depth of its crystal sphere the mutable reflections of the world and the revolutions of its hidden things; all designs full of mystical attraction and passion, of bitter sweetness and burning beauty.

Outside the immediate cycle of this legend of love divine and human, the artist has done much other work of a cognate kind; his sketches and studies in this line have always the charm of a visible enjoyment in the vigorous indulgence of a natural taste and power. One of these, a noble study of "Sleepers and One that Watches," has been translated into verse of kindred strength and delicacy, in three fine sonnets of high rank among the clear-cut and exquisite "Intaglios" of Mr. John Payne. But the artist is not a mere cloud-compeller, a dreamer on the wing who cannot use his feet for good travelling purpose on hard ground; witness the admirable picture of Roman ladies at a show of gladiators, exhibited in 1865, which remains still his masterpiece of large dramatic realism and live imagination. All the heads are full of personal force and character, especially the woman's with heavy brilliant hair and glittering white skin, like hard smooth snow against the sunlight, the delicious thirst and subtle ravin of sensual hunger for blood visibly enkindled in every line of the sweet fierce features. Mr. Solomon apparently has sufficient sense of physiology to share the theory which M. Alphonse Karr long since proposed to develope at length in a systematic treatise "sur la férocité des blondes." The whole spirit of this noble picture is imbued with the proper tragic beauty and truth and terror.

As the Hebrew love of dim vast atmosphere and infinite spiritual range without foothold on earth or resting-place in nature is perceptible in the mystic and symbolic cast of so many sketches and studies, so is a certain loving interest in the old sacred forms, in the very body of historic tradition, made manifest in various more literal designs of actual religious offices. One series of such represents on a small scale, with singular force and refinement, the several ceremonies of the sacred seasons and festivals of the Jewish year. Other instances of this ceremonial bias towards religious forms of splendour or solemnity are frequent in the list of the painter's works; gorgeous studies of eastern priests in church or synagogue, of young saint and rabbi and Greek bishop doing their divine service in "full blown dignity" of official magic. I remember faces among them admirable for holy heaviness of feature and sombre stolidity of sanctitude. No Venetian ever took truer delight in glorious vestures, in majestic embroideries, in the sharp deep sheen and glowing refraction of golden vessels; none of them ever lusted more hotly after the solid splendours of metal and marble, the grave glories of purple raiment and gleaming cup or censer. This same magnificence gives tone and colour to his classic subjects which explains their kinship to designs apparently so diverse in aim. Modern rather than classical, as we have noticed, in sentiment and significance, they combine the fervent violence of feeling or faith which is peculiar to the Hebrews with the sensitive acuteness of desire, the sublime reserve and balance of passion, which is peculiar to the Greeks. Something of Ezekiel is here mixed with something of Anacreon; here the Anthology and the Apocalypse have each set a distinct mark: the author of the Canticles and the author of the Atys have

agreed for a while to work together. The grievous and
glorious result of aspiration and enjoyment is here leg-
ible; the sadness that is latent in gladness; the pleasure
that is palpable in pain. Fixed eyes and fervent lips are
full of divine disquiet and instinctive resignation. All
the sorrow of the senses is incarnate in the mournful
and melodious beauty of those faces; they have learnt
to abstain from wishing; they are learning to abstain
from hope. Especially in such works as the "Sappho"
and the "Antinous" of some years since does this un-
conscious underlying sense assert itself. The wasted
and weary beauty of the one, the faultless and fruitful
beauty of the other, bear alike the stamp of sorrow;
of perplexities unsolved and desires unsatisfied. They
are not the divine faces familiar to us: the lean and
dusky features of this Sappho are unlike those of her
traditional bust, so clear, firm, and pure; this Antinous
is rather like Ampelus than Bacchus: But the heart
and soul of these pictures none can fail to recognise as
right; and the decoration is in all its details noble and
significant. The clinging arms and labouring lips of
Sappho, her fiery pallor and swooning eyes, the bitter
and sterile savour of subsiding passion which seems to
sharpen the mouth and draw down the eyelids, translate as far as colour can translate her. The face and
figure beside her are soulless and passive, the beauty
inert as a flower's; the violent spirit that aspires, the
satisfied body that takes rest, are here seen as it were
in types; the division of pure soul and of mere flesh;
the powerful thing that lives without peace, and the
peaceful thing that vegetates without power. In the

"Sacrifice of Antinous," he officiates before the god
under the divine disguise of Bacchus himself; the
curled and ample hair, the pure splendour of faultless
cheek and neck, the leopard-skin and thyrsus, are all
of the god, and godlike; the mournful wonderful lips
and eyes are coloured with mortal blood and lighted
with human vision.

In these pictures some obscure suppressed tragedy
of thought and passion and fate seems latent as the
vital veins under a clear skin. Intentionally or not as
it may be, some utter sorrow of soul, some world-old
hopelessness of heart, mixed with the strong sweet
sense of power and beauty, has here been cast afresh
into types. Elsewhere again, as in an earlier drawing
which my remembrance makes much of, this dim
tragic undertone is absent. The two ministering maidens in the Temple of Venus are priestesses of no sad
god, preachers of no sad thing. They have not seen
beyond the day's beauty, nor desired a delight beyond
the hour's capacity to give. As the Epithalamium of
Catullus to his Atys, so is this bright and sweet drawing to the Sappho. Here all is clear red and pale white,
the serene and joyful colours of pure marble and shed
rose-leaves: there dim green and shadows of dusky
gray surround and sadden the splendour of fair faces
and bright limbs. This artist affects soft backgrounds
of pale southern foliage and the sudden slim shoots of
a light southern spring; these often give the keynote to
his designs, always adding to them a general grace of
shape and gravity of tone as unmistakable as any other
special quality of work. But here nothing is deeper or

darker than the fallen petals which spot the fair pavement of the temple. One girl, white-robed and radiant as white water-flowers, has half let fall the rose that droops in her hand, dropping leaf by leaf like tears; both have the languor and the fruitful air of flowers in a sultry place; their leaning limbs and fervent faces are full of the goddess; their lips and eyes allure and await the invisible attendant Loves. The clear pearl-white cheeks and tender mouths have still about them the subtle purity of sleep; the whole drawing has upon it the heavy incumbent light of summer but half awake. Nothing of more simple and brilliant beauty has been done of late years. Here the spirit of joy is pure and whole; but a spirit more common is that which foresees with out eyes and forebears without ears the far-off features and the soundless feet of change; such a spirit as dictated the choice of subject in a picture of two young lovers in fresh fullness of first love crossed and troubled visibly by the mere shadow and the mere breath of doubt, the dream of inevitable change to come which dims the longing eyes of the girl with a ghostly foreknowledge that this too shall pass away, as with arms half clinging and half repellent she seems at once to hold off and to hold fast the lover whose bright youth for the moment is smiling back in the face of hers—a face full of the soft fear and secret certitude of future things which I have tried elsewhere to render in the verses called "Erotion" written as a comment on this picture, with design to express the subtle passionate sense of mortality in love itself which wells up from "the middle spring of pleasures," yet cannot

quite kill the day's delight or eat away with the bitter
poison of doubt the burning faith and self-abandoned
fondness of the hour; since at least, though the future
be for others, and the love now here turn elsewhere
to seek pasture in fresh fields from other flowers, the
vows and kisses of these his present lips are not theirs
but hers, as the memory of his love and the shadow of
his youth shall be hers for ever.

In such designs the sorrow is simple as the beauty,
the spirit simple as the form; in others there is all the
luxury and mystery of southern passion and eastern
dream. Many of these, as the figure bearing the eucha-
rist of love, have a supersexual beauty, in which the
lineaments of woman and of man seem blended as
the lines of sky and landscape melt in burning mist
of heat and light. Others, as the Bacchus, have about
them a fleshly glory of godhead and bodily deity,
which holds at once of earth and heaven; neither the
mystic and conquering Indian is this god, nor the
fierce choregus of Cithæron. The artist's passionate
love of gorgeous mysteries, "prodigious mixtures and
confusions strange" of sense and spirit no less than "of
good and ill," has given him the will and the power to
spiritualise at his pleasure, by the height and splendour
of his treatment, the somewhat unspiritual memory
of Heliogabalus, "Emperor of Rome and High Priest
of the Sun," symbolic in that strange union of offices
at once of east and west, of ghostly glory and visible
lordship, of the lusts of the flesh and the secrets of the
soul, of the kingdom of this world and the mystery of
another: the superb and luxurious power and subtle-

ty of the study take in both aspects of his figure, the strangest surely that ever for an instant overtopped the world.

There is an entire class of Mr. Solomon's designs in which the living principle and moving spirit is music made visible. His groups of girls and youths that listen to one singing or reciting seem utterly imbued with the spirit of sound, clothed with music as with a garment, kindled and swayed by it as fire or as foliage by a wakening wind. In pictures where no one figures as making music, the same fine inevitable sense of song makes melodies of vocal colour and symphonies of painted cadence. The beautiful oil painting of bride, bridegroom, and paranymph has in its deep ripe tones the same suffusion of sound as that of the evening hymn to the hours; the colours have speech in them, a noble and solemn speech, and full of large strong harmonies. In the visible "mystery of faith" we feel the same mighty measures of a silent song go up with the elevation of the host; and from the soundless lips of Love and Sleep, of Memory and of Dreams, of Pleasure and Lust and Death, the voice of their manifold mystery is audible

In almost all of these there is perceptible the same profound suggestion of unity between opposites, the same recognition of the identity of contraries. Even in the gatherings of children about the knees of Love, as he tells his first tales to elder and younger lads and girls, there are touches of trouble and distraction, of faint doubt and formless pain on the fresh earnest faces that attend in wonder and in trance. Even in the glad soft grouping of boys and maidens by "summer twilight," under light bloom of branches that play against a gracious gleaming sky, their clear smiles and swift chance gestures recall some thought of the shadow as well as the light of life; and always there seems to rise up before the spirit, at thought of the might and ravage of time and "sad mortality," the eternal question—

> How with this rage shall beauty hold a plea,
> Whose action is no stronger than a flower?

But far other questions than this rise up behind it, as we gaze into the great and terrible mystery of beauty, and turn over in thought the gloss of far other commentators, the scrolls of strange interpreters, materialist and mystic. In the features of these groups and figures which move and make music before us in the dumb show of lines and colours, we see the latent relations of pain and pleasure, the subtle conspiracies of good with evil, the deep alliances of death and life, of love and hate, of attraction and abhorrence. Whether suffering or enjoyment be the master expression of a face, and whether that enjoyment or that suffering be merely or mainly spiritual or sensual, it is often hard to say—hard often to make sure whether the look of loveliest features be the look of a cruel or a pitiful soul. Sometimes the sensible vibration as of living lips and eyes lets out the secret spirit, and we see the springs of its inner and confluent emotions. The subtleties and harmonies of suggestion in such studies of complex or it may be perverse nature would have drawn forth praise and sympathy from Baudelaire, most loving of all students of strange beauty and abnormal refinement, of painful pleasures of soul and inverted raptures of sense. There is a mixture of utmost delicacy with a fine cruelty in some of these faces of fair feminine youth which recalls the explanation of a philosopher of the material school, whose doctrine is at least not without historic example and evidence to support it: "Une infinité de sots, dupes de cette incroyable sensibilité qu'ils voient dans les femmes, ne se doutent pas que les extrémités se rapprochent, et que c'est précisemént au foyer de ce sentiment que la cruauté prend sa source. Parce que *la cruauté n'est elle-même qu'une des branches de la sensibilité*, et que c'est toujours en raison du degré dont nos âmes en sont pénétrées que les grandes horreurs se commettent." The matter of this passage is better than the style; by the presence of this element we may distinguish cruelty from brutality, a Nero from a Gallifet, a Brinvilliers from a "baby-farmer." In several of Mr. Solomon's designs we find heads emblematic of active or visionary passion upon which the seal of this sensitive cruelty is set; made beautiful beyond the beauty of serpent or of tiger by the sensible infusion of a soul which refines to a more delicate delight the mere nervous lust after blood, the mere physical appetite and ravenous relish for fleshly torture; which finds out the very "spirit of sense" and fine root of utmost feeling alike in the patient and the agent of the pain. There are no bestial faces, no mere vile types of brutality, but only of this cunning and cruel sensibility which catches fire from the stroke it deals, and drinks as its wine of life the blood of its sentient sacrifice. The poignancy of this pleasure is patent and fervent in the face of the fair woman overlooking the fresh full agony in the circus; the aftertaste of fierce weariness and bitter languor that corrodes the soul is perceptible in the aspect of the figure representing Lust, with haunted eyes and savage haggard lips and barren body scored with blood, in the allegoric design of Love. Other faces again are live emblems of an infinite tenderness, of sad illimitable pity, of the sweetness of utter faith and ardour that consumes all the meaner elements of life; the fiery passion and hunger after God of St. Theresa, who might be taken as patroness of the Christian side of this painter's art: one whole class of his religious designs is impregnated with the burning mysticism and raging rapture of her visions, reflected as we feel them in Crashaw's hymn of invocation from the furnace of her own fierce words and phrases of prostrate ardour and amorous appeal to her Bridegroom.

All great and exquisite colourists have a mystery of their own, the conscience of a power known to themselves only as the heart knows its own bitterness, and not more communicable or explicable. In this case the pictorial power is so mixed with personal quality, so informed and suffused with a subtle energy of sentiment, that a student from without may perhaps be able to note, not quite inaccurately or unprofitably, the main spiritual elements of the painter's work. In the work of some artists the sentiment is either a blank or a mist; and none but technical criticism of such work can be other than incompetent and injurious. The art of Mr. Solomon is of a kind which has inevitable attraction for artists of another sort, and is all the more liable to suffer from the verdicts of unskilled and untrained judgments. But an artist of his rank and quality has no need to cry out against the rash intrusion of critical stragglers from the demesne of any other art. He can afford the risk of such sympathies, for his own is rich in the qualities of those others also, in musical and poetic excellence not less positive than the pictorial; and as artist he stands high enough to be above all chance of the imputation cast on some that they seek comfort in the ignorant admiration and reciprocal sympathy of men who cultivate some alien line of art, for conscious incompetence and failure in their own; fain to find shelter for bad painting under the plea of poetic feeling, or excuse for bad verse under the plea of good thought or sentiment. By right of his innate energies and actual performances, he claims kinship and alliance with the foremost in all fields of art, while holding in his own a special and memorable place. Withdrawn from the roll of artists, his name would leave a void impossible to fill up by any worthiest or ablest substitute; by any name of master in the past or disciple in the present or future. The one high test requisite for all genuine and durable honour is beyond all question his; he is himself alone, and one whose place no man can take. They only, but they assuredly, of whom this can be said, may trust in their life to come. Time wears out the names of the best imitators and followers; but he whose place is his own, and that place high among his fellows, may be content to leave his life's work with all confidence to time.

LETTERS FROM
SIMEON SOLOMON TO
ALGERNON CHARLES SWINBURNE

Sept 30

My dear Wise,

The enclosed letters from Simeon Solomon contain direct references to his notorious vices, and an indication that A.C.S. was quite aware of their nature. I therefore suggest to you that they should be destroyed at once, if you agree. I have kept another note of S.S. which is quite innocuous and has an interesting feature.

Ever yours,
Edmund Gosse

[September 1869]

12 Fitzroy Street, W.

My dear Swinburne,

I am so sorry I missed you the other morning when you called. I very much desired to see you and say how pleased I was to hear from Powell that you had been so well when you were away and that you had enjoyed your travels so well. I believe you did not make a long stay at Ste. Marie des Bois, but under the circumstances I can understand it; I heard indirectly of "notre chere orphelin" as something of her that I confess pained, nay, shocked me.

How long do you remain away, but I suppose some time as you are at home. I sincerely hope a book will soon transpire. What do you think? a model called Miss Blake who is one of your most devoted admirers ran off with the copy of *Poems and Ballads* that you gave me, and nothing has been heard of her or it: I fear that she has changed her mode of life for the worse, but I hope against fear. I send you by book post a volume just published by a friend of mine called Davies, he gave it me for you yesterday. Both he and I are anxious to hear your opinion *and* a tremendously good notice has appeared in the *Examiner*. I think some of the sonnets are charming. Have you heard that Capell is going to publish a popular "Justine"? We are coming to a sense of what is right. Send me a little letter.

With love,
Ever yours,
S. Solomon

[September 1869]

Saracen's Head,
Beddgelert,
Carnavonshire,

My dear Swinburne,

Really I feel so divided between flattered vanity and anger that I hardly know what to say to you; the first in a great degree on account of your telling me that my letter was interesting, (I feared it was horribly dull,) and anger that you should fill a letter and spend so much time on me about a subject which, I regarded with the deepest and most unqualified horror not unmixed with feelings of deep commiseration!!!! I assure you that I wept at the recital of the boyish agonies you depicted in your last, I was doubled up with grief at the idea of so many tender posteriors quivering under the pitiless strokes of the rod, swayed, doubtless, by a man not wholly free from faults himself, but enough of a subject from which I avert my mental and physical eyes.

My friend, who has excited so much sympathy and interest in your breast, is called William Eden Nesfield, he is the son of a water colour painter and landscape gardener of no unenviable fame (vide *Modern Painters*, I forget which volume) and he, the former, is one of our very best architects, a man of great knowledge, invention, and consummate amiability. He is a fat, jolly hearty fellow, genuinely good natured, very fond of smoking, and I deeply grieve to say of women; although doubtless bearing the marks of the many Etonian rods I mentioned, feels no more the *real* merit and meaning of that instrument of delight than my pen does; I should unhesitatingly pronounce him to be not at all of a sensual temperament in your and my conception of the term; the way in which the subject was brought up was as follows. I had bought a week or two before I saw him a penny paper of no merit whatever, called *Peter Spy*, exceedingly coarse, silly, and unsatisfactory but the week I bought it there happened to be a picture on the first page, which, though not in a first rate style of art, was sufficiently to purchase for the mean sum of a penny. The subject treated was entitled "THE DISGRACEFUL ACT OF FLAGELLATION FROM THE EARLIEST AGES TO THE PRESENT TIME," at least as far as I can remember that was the title. The picture represented a young girl in a highly resigned condition unlacing her stays, she was represented with an exceedingly large crinoline and a very small waist, on one side of her was a shameless libertine of advanced age, and of noble rank, holding in one hand a rod (I draw much better ones) and in the other a rope, wherewith to lash the fair young victim to a step ladder in the background, on the other side of the poor young girl was drawn an elderly woman of unprepossessing appearance also holding a rod and a rope—on the ground were represented what many of my friends assure me were D-LD-O. The scene is a most inelegantly furnished bedroom; but enough of the description. The article is poorly written but somewhat interesting. I believe the paper has been suppressed. I have kept it to show you when you come to see me. Well, as I was saying, I showed it to Nesfield, and naturally the subject of rods turned up, whereupon he gave up the account of his flagellation that I described in my last; it will be by no means difficult for you to meet him, for his rooms are in Argyll Street near mine, and he has a very jolly collection of Persian, Indian, Greek and Japanese things that I should really like you to see, so, if you care to go, I will take you round to him when you call upon me, he is an intimate friend of Albert Moore. I have known him a long time: by the way, I showed the paper of which I have been speaking to Moore and when he read it he asked me with open mouth and eyes what it meant; he was entirely ignorant on the whole subject, and I sighed to think how I was in his happy, innocent condition before I knew a certain poet whom I will forbear to mention, but I warrant you, I quickly enlightened him. Your letter came to me in such an atmosphere of virtue that I assure you it had the effect of a thunderbolt. When the servant gave it me I was holding a spirited and earnest conversation with Holiday's brother on the excellence of benevolent societies am the abstract question of philanthropy: I left them (the community of Saints) yesterday and I shall return to London on Thursday: I began yester-day evening here, pour m'amuser, the autobiography of a man of irregular affections. I will give you a few extracts you will observe that I do not sympathise entirely with the wretched victim of passion which I blush and tremble to name, which as the charming Dr. Lempriere would say, "might call a blush upon the cheek of the most abandoned."

"I should doubtless be rigorously judged by two widely different classes of my fellow men, namely, those whose passionless temperaments are incapable of being excited by anything in heaven above or in the earth beneath, or if you will allow me the expression, in the hell beneath the earth; the other class is composed of those persons, and their name is legion, who find a delight in visiting casinos, and other dull, disreputable resorts of the like nature, and an amusement, nay, a satisfaction in copulating with vulgar and often diseased persons of the opposite sex."

"Virtuous persons of the first class I have named would doubtless deplore my irregular propensities, while vicious persons of the next class would probably hate me for them; I am indifferent to both; pity would not melt, and obloquy would not change me."

"I will at once candidly unbosom to my readers, my affections are divided between the boy and the birch; I think it is neither necessary or important here to say which has the greater portion of my swelling heart, perhaps the division has been equal for, although I have always felt an inexpressible and thrilling pleasure in the company and confidence of handsome boys, these without that instrument of flagellant delights have not completely satisfied. There has been a sensible void: I have yearned for something more: time was, when this yearning was undefined, I did not know that it was the rod I burned for: . . ."

"On the other hand, the rod, radiant and blooming as it is with flowers of Love has never yielded me the true joy when separated from the blushing bottom which Providence has destined to receive its strokes. . . ."

"With regard to my wife, I sincerely trust shall treat her kindly and justly, I do not fear that I shall prove faithless."

Extracted from an MS autobiography of
A—Z—

Being completely ashamed of myself and having I should imagine tired you sufficiently I shall, mv dear Swinburne, bid you good bye. On my return I will make you many drawings[1]. I remain

Yours sincerely,
Simeon Solomon

P.S. Moore and I came to the conclusion that the drawing in *Peter Spy* was made by a man who is accustomed to draw patterns of books, for the books as you will see are eminently superior to the rest of the drawing.

---

1 In the bottom left-hand corner of the letter, beneath the postscript, is a small ink sketch by Solomon depicting a crowned female figure in profile presenting a bundle of birth-twigs to a kneeling man as other figures lurk in the background bearing the legend *The Queen presenting rods to the school-masters of the United Kingdom.*

[November 1869]

Arts Club,
Hanover Square

My dear Swinburne,

I really ought to have written to you before this after having received such an elegant and improving epistle as yours was to me, but you know how one defers these things. I have often wanted to see you and I hope you will now soon be coming to London. I suppose you have been leading a perfectly idyllic life at home. Has it been chequered or shall I say enlivened, by any more interesting young cousins? I have tried to find out who your friend of the honourable wounds was but as you did not tell me his name I have not been able to do so.

Did I tell you that I saw Powell when he was here and that he carried off a little picture of mine that I painted in Rome? I have had it photographed and I write a line under it from *Hermaphroditus* "Love turned himself and would not enter in." I have had great fun lately with a little French model who sits to me by me telling her to ask different people for *Justine* which I assure her she ought to peruse with care. She has learned some of the choicest expressions from that great book. I want you to see what I am painting now, it is the "Summer Twilight." You remember the photo of it probably. I think it will turn out well; I am painting it for a most charming little clergy-man, one who unites religious unction with the broadest aesthetic views. Chapman has just been painting the portrait of his wife. I want to know what you think of Pater's article in the *Fortnightly*. I like much of it immensely, but I think it unequal, the description of Monna Lisa is delightful—I went to see him at Oxford a little time since. I want to regale you with a pretty little story. A young friend of mine at Oxford wrote to ask me if I would object to his writing an article on my drawings &c. I replied that I should feel much flattered—a few days afterwards I got a letter from him asking me if I would be kind enough to explain the meanings of them—isn't that charming? Have you heard of the new Art Magazine that is about to happen—it is to be called the "Portfolio" a bad name I think, but otherwise it promises not badly. There are to be autograph copies of drawings by the leading artists of the day, with appropriate articles appended to them. I believe the thing is to be modelled on the principle of the *Gazette des Beaux Arts*—it is a thing very much wanted as we have nothing at all of the kind in England. I had such a shocking dream the other night. I dreamed that a cat and a sheep had connection and the hideous offspring appeared a few minutes after the event, it was a little black creature with long nails of wire which fastened into me, and as I pulled them out they became alive like worms, wasn't that shocking? Have you seen what they said about in the Saturday? How it was their duty to urge me to have more respect for Christian feeling &c it was most amusing. I fear I have nothing of any interest to tell you of, I wish I had. This letter is merely

a sign that I have been thinking about you and to say
how glad I am and others will be to see you in London
again. Write if you have an opportunity.

Ever affectionately yours,
S. Solomon

P.S. The fervent Catholic tone of your letter
touched me extremely. I could hardly resist showing
it to Sister Letitia who would have had an ecstasy on
the spot for *all* the new orders of which you speak and
which were hitherto unknown in the Catholic world,
and the soul restoring office of the Exposition of the
Eve Blessed.

[Late February 1870]

12 Fitzroy Street, S.W.

My dear Swinburne

How can I sufficiently thank you for the very
charming ballad you sent me on Friday? I was delighted with it and I deeply regret that I could not read it
all at home, however what I did read was duly appreciated. It is very satisfactory to know that the civility
was written by the Bishop of London although you
give his G another name. Have you done any more to
the Carol which delighted me very much, every one
has been asking me if I am in possession of the whole

of it, but I am not aware that you have written any more.

Are you ever coming to London again? It seems not certainly, but no doubt you know what is best and most agreeable for you to do. I did not see Powell at all in town, which I extremely regretted. Please do not consider this a letter at all, it is simply and acknowledgement of your sweet literary presents to me. Do come to town soon and solace your affectionate friend.

S. Solomon

[May 1, 1871]

Care of Colonel Brine,
Shaldon, Teignmouth.

My dear Swinburne

I am happy to say that your letter reached me and was not lost on its way and opened and read by the authorities of the P.O. Alas! what would have been the consequences? We dare not, indeed, surmise. I was pleased to hear from you but grieved at what your letter conveyed to me. I can hardly believe it, but yet after your learned manner of accounting for the existence of the unfortunate young person, I am persuaded to do so—she (is it feminine?) should at once be sent to a conventional establishment and be taken under the strictest supervisions—she should wear an acolyte next the skin and never bath without a warm celebrant (to be procured at every respectable chemist.) I asked the lady at whose house I was staying if she had heard of the book—she said she had heard of Lady Blake, and with good taste and tact denied knowledge of anything further. Your eloquence on the subject was so great that I must "with a blush retire."

Are you in town? I return at the end of the week. I find Devonshire and the sea lovely. I am staying with a great admirer of yours and have read most of your *Songs before Sunrise* to her. I have also been staying with another admirer at Torquay, Miss Annie Thomas the novelist now Mrs. Pendercudlip (I beg to state that *I* did not pend her cudlip, I would scorn the action), let me know where you are and will be. I shall be in London by Sunday next, the 7th.

Yours affectionately,
S. Solomon

[May, 1871]

12 Fitzroy Street, W.

My dear Swinburne

What a wonderful letter was your last to me! I hardly dare to reply to it for how can I render you sufficient thanks? The last part was perhaps the most brilliant of all—I died over it. The transposition of the syllables was quite worthy of your humorous powers, and can I say fairer than that I have heard a great deal of the Dolomites, but I thank my maker that *I* have never, never zigzagged (what a difficult word to write!) among them, no, I have not fallen as low as that. They are north of Venice and considered very fine—all you say is quite true and just and evinces your keen sense of right and wrong. This is a naughty world and its naughtiness is not concealed just now—the zigzaggs (damn the word) of certain young persons are falling on their own heads, if such an event be possible.

I grieve to say that I lost your first letter, but you need not fear that it will be found, but if it were to be, I hope it would be quite appreciated. I want to ask you a favour, which I hope you will at once refuse or comply with, as you think proper. I want to know if you will write a little article about my book in connection with my pictures, *etc.* I remember your saying that if I ever published it you would say something about it. I should so much like you to do so, and I will do thing anything for you, (des supplices, des supplices). I am sending a copy the *Dark Blue* and if you comply, I will at once let the magazine to know. I am sure it would do me good, I am not just now doing anything very brilliant and it would be sure to direct people's attention thing to my things—, but of course at the same time I do not reckon on your complying but of course leave it entirely to your inclination. Will you let me have a line soon? Yes, many, many lines.

I am so glad you are so much better. I wish you were always as well in London; are you working on Tristram or Bothwell, or both—I read all your *Songs before Sunrise*[1] to Mrs. Brine, and I certainly LIKE them (most of them) better than anything else of yours, especially "The Eve of Revolution" and "Siena". The latter is absolutely perfect and lovely.

I hear there is a new American poet, what do you think of him? I have not yet seen his work. I hope I shall see much of you in London and I hope more that you will not try your health so much when you come.

Ever truly yours,
S. Solomon

[May, 1871]

12 Fitzroy Street, W.

My dear Swinburne

Many thanks for your kindness. I have just sent a letter to the editor of the *Dark Blue* telling him of your offer and suggesting that it might be in the June number and as I know how swiftly you write, I think that would be possible, would it not? it is today only the 15th. (I hope I have done nothing in bad taste in

---

1 Instead of writing the phrase "Sunrise" in the title of Swinburne's recent collection Solomon draws a semi-circle with rays extending off the upper edge

thus writing to the D.B. (O, monsieur) but if I don't
look after myself no one will do it for me.)] I cannot tell
you what pleasure it will give me to see something by
you on me (that sounds rather improper) and in print.
I suppose the editor will communicate with you.

Your letter is delightful and I could not tell you
much, for on Friday I was taken by Hurt's counsel to
the trial. There were some very funny things said but
nothing improper except the disgusting and silly med-
ical evidence of which I heard but very little. Reynolds
publishes everything and the D.T. does nearly the
same. I think the public interest has quite died away. I
saw the writer of those highly effusive letters, he looks
rather humdrum certainly. Oddly enough after the
morning trial when I left, of course I was ravenous
and went to the nearest restaurant where I found Bn,
Pk, and H at lunch with their solicitors. Karslak the
solicitor and I sat down with them, which, as it was
a public crowded room I had no hesitation in doing.
Bn is very remarkable, he is not quite beautiful but
supremely pretty, a perfect figure, manner and voice.
Although I was agreeably surprised at him. Of course
they will be acquitted. I am so glad to be able to relieve
your mind with regard to your first letter. I did destroy
it, but I thought you would think it a very poor com-
pliment to do so, so I did not like telling you. I quite
appreciate your story about the chorister. I will write
soon again and thanking you much believe me,

Ever affectionaly yours,

S. Solomon

[May 1871]

12 Fitzroy S.

My dear Swinburne

I have just received your letter and think all you say is quite right and certainly very pleasing and flattering to me. You may be sure that the longer and fuller what you write will be the more advantage it will give me; I have just written to Freund giving him the substance of your letter (not the whole of it) and I said that if your MSS. did not arrive in time for insertion—I thought he might put a little critical advice of the "vision" at the end of the number as he thought of doing because I said that you would probably speak of my pictures and drawings and use the booklet only as a sort of accompaniment, I hope I did right?—but I should think he would not put a notice in at all, as he would think that you would more than exhaust the subject. May I mention a few of my things that I should like you to think of? I painted the Antinous Dionysius 6 years ago. There was nothing improper about it. Then I did "Habet" and that picture you wrote a poem about "Erotion". You know all my sketches I think "Love and Lust", Sleep and Charity", then my Dudley Gallery things. "Bacchus", "Greek Bishop", "Heliogabalus", "Sacramentum Amoris", "Youthful Eastern Saint", "A Song", "Group of Girls

and Youths", "One Girl Singing", "Summer Twilight",
"Young Rabbi"—then I had an oil picture of the
"Bride and friend of the Bridegroom" and lastly "The
Evening Hymn to the Lovers" one of my best things
for color I think. Now I have "Mystery of Faith",
"Priest Blessing the Host", and the drawings "Singing
of Love", "Love's Sleep", "Memory Dreams Pleasures
Lust and Death", but your memory is so tremendous
that you always seem to retain everything you have
once seen or heard.

I will not bore you any more by correspondence on
this subject. I think it is arranged now and I cannot do
better than leave it in your hands and make no more
suggestions. You never have anything in the *Fortnightly*
now, how is this? I miss your contributions greatly.

I have a model waiting so I must send this off at
once; I will soon write again and if I can an amusing
letter, but I suppose you will be soon in Town.

Affecly yr's
S. Solomon

[May 1871]

[Address not given]

My dear Swinburne,

10,000,000 thanks for your great kindness—it is
really too good of you to have occupied so much of
your time for so unworthy an object but the result is

splendid—I have told Freund that he must not omit any part of it, for it is so complete and finished that it must be delayed till the July number if it be too long for this; I am sure you will agree in this, for you would not desire or even permit your work to be clipped. I have only one fault to find and that is that you much overrate my capacity; my sentiment is a gift, no credit to me, but my work, alas! is below your estimate of it, however it seems so ungrateful to comment even upon what you have done that I will desist—this is merely a grateful acknowledgement of what you have sent—I will write again and tell you more of Cecil who is without exception one of the naughtiest boys I ever knew; could you guess what he did the other day? but no, I will not create fresh prejudices against him—

Ever yours affly
S. Solomon

[October 1871]

18 John Street, Bedford Row

My dear Swinburne

I received your letter of yesterday and I am very sorry to find from its tone that what I said in mine must have been very awkwardly and ungraciously done. It is very difficult for me to know what to say to you but I am quite sure that whatever I may say

will not imply a want of gratitude for and acknowl-
edgment of your kindness in writing the article in
the *Dark Blue*. And you must promise to forgive me
if I speak the whole truth about it. When you sent
the M.S. and I read it, I saw and appreciated the full
beauty of the paper and the great honour that had
been done me by the most brilliant of our writers,
but I saw that there were certain parts which I could
have desired to be omitted but I dared not ask you
to eliminate or even to modify them, for I thought it
would have been a liberty, and, as a beggar who had
so large a boon conferred upon him, I felt it would
have been unjustifiable: when the article appeared in
print one or two very intimate friends said "eloquent
and beautiful as it is, I think it will do you harm". You
know, of course, my dear Algernon, that, by many,
my designs and pictures executed during the last three
or four years have been looked upon with suspicion,
and, as I have been a false friend to myself, I have not
sought to remove the impression, but I have gone on
following my own sweet will; in pecuniary and some
other ways I have had to suffer for it, and shall probably have to suffer still. I really hardly know how to say
any more, but I wish to make you feel that what I said
in my last letter and what I repeat in this arises from
no want of gratitude for the honour you did me and
the kindness you showed me and I hope you will send
me a letter absolving me from such an imputation in
your mind.

Ever affectionately yours,

S.S.

[October, 1871]

[Address not given]

My dear Algernon,

I was so pleased and relieved by your last letter and the kind manner in which you so completely exonerated me from the charge of ingratitude and ungraciousness; I saw by it that you entirely understood what I meant although it was awkwardly conveyed; I cannot at this moment call to mind the precise passages which I felt I should have liked modified but if it be worthwhile I will try to do so when I see you which I hope will be soon; I think, disagreeable as it is for me to have to do so, that in much of my (slighter) work I have given grounds for the kind of remarks that have been made. I intend now to go in for a different kind of work and cultivate that element that was more prominent some years ago, I mean the dramatic (on the intellectual side) and the effective (on the artistic side.) I have a little picture in the Dudley of a synagogue which really I think is liked more than anything I have ever done, I should like you to see it and to learn what you think of it?

Had I seen Poynter the other evening and he told me he had enjoyed his 3 weeks travel greatly, I may go up to the Grange shortly. I looked at the *Contemporary* and certainly it is the silliest and feeblest of any arti-

cle of that kind I ever saw, but it is so weak that it
does not merit the delightful bit of indignation you
bestowed upon it at the end of your last letter. It is *not*
by Buchannan though he is no doubt capable of it.

A. Moore showed me the first edition of Notre
Orphelin the other day, it had no plates, save for one
of the boy singing in the pseudo-Rafael style of the
15th century which had so little merit—you are out
of the beastly fogs which are ravishing us here and
preventing the practice of our delightful art. I meet
the Scotts on Saturday. Laetita was unwell, the poor
dear! I am going to see them soon. I wish you would
tell me what you are doing, I should very much like
to know.

I remain,
Very truly yours,
S. Solomon.

[November 1872]

[Address not given]

Dear Swinburne,

If you send a letter to the Savile Club, Savile Row,
it will reach S C as he is there nearly every day. He
will be delighted to receive your offering and of course
will do all you want with regard to forwarding it to its
right destination. I am very sorry that you have been

suffering so much, but this weather will account for every thing; here it rains almost unceasingly. I went to Eton last week for a couple of days, but the weather was dreadful; have you heard that Johnson has left and changed his name to Corry, it is creating a sensation at Eton. I suppose you will be in town about Christmas.

Believe me,
Yours ever,
S. Solomon

[November 1872]

12 Fitzroy Street

My dear Algernon,

I enclose a letter from Colvin, the contents of which, as he says, will no doubt interest you—I thought I should have heard from you and have almost felt that you must have had some (I hope, slight) cause of annoyance with me, but I trust that is not the case. I was heartily glad when I called at your rooms and found you had left London, for I must frankly say that I think that the only course for you as regards health and comfort, but I also hope that you will be and remain well in your new rooms which I consider charming—George Powell has been at great pains to do your behests—his quest of the Tragedy of Arden was worthy of a knight of the round table, but success,

as I daresay you will know by this time, has crowned
his efforts—he is very unselfish and only happy when
he is doing some service for others.

I remain

always truly yours

S. Solomon

P.S. I have had many enquiries after you. I spent
the evening with two friends of mine a little since,
the Misses Forbes who told me they had met some
members of your family at a house in Scotland and
expressed a great wish to see you.

A PARTIAL LIST OF SNUGGLY BOOKS

ETHEL ARCHER *The Hieroglyph*
G. ALBERT AURIER *Elsewhere and Other Stories*
CHARLES BARBARA *My Lunatic Asylum*
CHARLES BARBARA *Stirring Stories*
S. HEZOLNRY BERTHOUD *Misanthropic Tales*
LÉON BLOY *The Tarantulas' Parlor and Other Unkind Tales*
ÉLÉMIR BOURGES *The Twilight of the Gods*
ADA BUISSON *The Baron's Coffin and Other Disquieting Tales*
CYRIEL BUYSSE *The Aunts*
JAMES CHAMPAGNE *Harlem Smoke*
FÉLICIEN CHAMPSAUR *The Latin Orgy*
ARMAND CHARPENTIER
    Claustrophobic Madness and Other Stories of Death and Love
BRENDAN CONNELL *Metrophilias*
BRENDAN CONNELL *Spells*
RENDAN CONNELL (editor) *The Zaffre Book of Occult Fiction*
BRENDAN CONNELL (editor) *The Zinzolin Book of Occult Fiction*
RAFAELA CONTRERAS *The Turquoise Ring and Other Stories*
DANIEL CORRICK (editor)
    Ghosts and Robbers: An Anthology of German Gothic Fiction
ADOLFO COUVE *When I Think of My Missing Head*
RENÉ CREVEL *Are You All Crazy?*
QUENTIN S. CRISP *Aiaigasa*
QUENTIN S. CRISP *Rule Dementia!*
LUCIE DELARUE-MARDRUS *The Last Siren and Other Stories*
LADY DILKE *The Outcast Spirit and Other Stories*
CATHERINE DOUSTEYSSIER-KHOZE *The Beauty of the Death Cap*
ÉDOUARD DUJARDIN *Hauntings*
BERIT ELLINGSEN *Now We Can See the Moon*
ERCKMANN-CHATRIAN *A Malediction*
ALPHONSE ESQUIROS *The Enchanted Castle*
ENRIQUE GÓMEZ CARRILLO *Sentimental Stories*
DELPHI FABRICE *Flowers of Ether*
DELPHI FABRICE *The Red Sorcerer*
DELPHI FABRICE *The Red Spider*
BENJAMIN GASTINEAU *The Reign of Satan*
EDMOND AND JULES DE GONCOURT *Manette Salomon*
REMY DE GOURMONT *From a Faraway Land*
REMY DE GOURMONT *Morose Vignettes*
GUIDO GOZZANO *Alcina and Other Stories*
GUSTAVE GUICHES *The Modesty of Sodom*
EDWARD HERON-ALLEN *The Complete Shorter Fiction*
EDWARD HERON-ALLEN *Three Ghost-Written Novels*